They Still Shoot
Models My Age

They Still Shoot Models My Age

SUSAN MONCUR

Library of Congress Catalog Card Number: 91-61198

British Library Cataloguing-in-Publication Data

Moncur, Susan
    They still shoot models my age
    I. Title
    920
ISBN 1-85242-230-0

The right of Susan Moncur to be identified as author
of this work has been asserted by her in accordance
with the Copyright, Designs and Patents Act 1988

Copyright © 1991 by Susan Moncur

First published 1991 by
Serpent's Tail, 4 Blackstock Mews, London N4

Set in 11/13pt Sabon by AKM Associates (UK) Ltd, London
Printed by Cox & Wyman Ltd of Reading, Berkshire

*To Sarah, Anna and
Jean-Noël*

With many thanks to Serge Lutens for use of cover photograph and for twenty years of work, music and laughter.

> 'Yeah . . . yeah, I still work,' says Susan, as surprised as if she'd just seen a chicken with teeth. 'But these are my last hours . . . my swan song. And I don't know what I'm going to do.'
> Interview by Fabian Gastellier, *L'Unité*.

Bill Rope has been modeling for thirty years, which is very rare. Long modeling careers can turn into a solitary search for something to do, able to do nothing though you've mimed most things.

Bill will be sixty this year. He just spent seven years in Missouri, taking care of an old aunt who lived alone on a farm. Long modeling careers can also turn you into a good Samaritan. You feel you should pay back some of the luxury you've enjoyed for so many years for no other reason than the way you look. And the emptiness it leaves you with must be filled. Good deeds are good filler.

Bill sent a photograph of himself and his aunt to a friend of his in Paris. I saw it. The odd couple, side by side. He's six foot four. She came up to just above Bill's belt.

His aunt died last September and Bill went traveling: New York, Los Angeles, Paris, trying to decide what to do, where to settle down. He's in Paris at the moment, and we worked together as extras on a commercial. Bill portrayed a horseman and I was 'Mrs Dalloway', with three bloodhounds on a leash. We were standing next to each other practically all day, pretending to be watching a parade. We talked, in between him calming his horse and me my dogs.

'When I was modeling more, people used to call the agency and ask: "Can he ski? Can he fly a plane?" They didn't know what to say. I can't do anything. They finally started saying it – "No, he can't do anything, but he *looks* like he can do *everything*."' Bill looks like a friendly distinguished diplomat who's always played sports.

'People say I could be a *maître d'hôtel*, or a wine waiter, but I know nothing about wine. People always chose it for me. I like it red and dry, that's all I know. If I'm eating alone in a restaurant, people will come up to me and ask me to choose their wine. I look like I know. Or waiting on the corner of the Boulevard St Germain for the *Herald Tribune* to arrive, – it arrives around midnight – people come up to me and ask for directions in all languages. I point.'

He said that a mutual friend of ours who had a house near Toulouse had invited him to live there all year round. That the friend spent only two months there in the summer, Bill could take care of it the rest of the time. Be the caretaker, although the friend had been careful not to use that word. Maybe he would do that because the weather was so nice.

'A good model should be permanently high; three or four glasses of champagne high.'

52 Minutes on the First,
a television documentary on the modeling profession.

I was never the one who suggested bed finally. I never wanted to go to bed. The after-work dinners, a drunken camaraderie already established. A mail-order catalog, *Vogue*, it never really matters. Being photographed.

Milan, October 27, 1978: Drinking champagne since eleven this morning. Everyone's trying to be funny. Maybe everyone is. Everyone's after someone's ass. Stomach hurting from laughing too much all day.

We go on after work to the Tower of Pisa, a late-night restaurant. No one's affair is arranged yet. Red and white wine, grappa and dirty jokes, leaning on each other.

Me and Beatrice take a pee together. You end up doing everything together. We bring an empty wine bottle into the john with us, pee in it, yellow-white wine – bring it back to the table and stuff it with bits off plates, order everyone to go pee in the bottle. But not everyone does. Aiming is too difficult.

I go outside and knock on the window next to our table. When the curtain is pulled aside, I yank my T-shirt up around my neck, pretending to strangle myself with it, not only for the benefit of our table but of the entire restaurant. Why do I crave to spread out like jelly on bread, so everyone can see everything?

I will have an affair with a man in the group. He's married, they're almost always married, but I don't mind. Love is war and I always lose, so who cares if there's another woman? Sometimes I don't mind losing, you might even say that I win, and sometimes it's a death rehearsal. In any case you learn how to fuck, for the pleasure. In case you don't naturally know how.

Paris June 1, 1983: Three o'clock in the afternoon, the worst part of the day, the middle. The worst part of my life, the middle? It's always the end of the record these days. I find the courage to put one on then and am too nervous to listen to it. Even mood music is cacophony but I keep trying. I pace, on my way to do something I've forgotten, re-heat coffee and settle down, I'm just tired, and the record ends again. I hate the needle turning, using itself up for nothing, as I do, but I let it turn for a while. It takes enormous energy to bend down and push the buttons. The stereo is badly placed, too low. I've never figured it out since I bought it, a year ago. I push the buttons till they work. I lift off the record arm which is too lightweight for my brittle aiming and it goes flying, scratching the record. I can't decide what else to play and I'm sick of what I've just heard as if in a half-forgotten dream.

Therapist tomorrow. Pay to talk so I won't bother my friends. Except I bother them. Not sure she's ideal. It seems improper to talk to a plain, plump woman about the end of a career in beauty.

Paris, June 15, 9.30 in the morning: Will call this episode of my career, beating a dead horse. The metro car is swerving like a drunken snake. Bought myself the consolation prize of this violet fine-tip felt pen. In my head, the conversation with M. yesterday afternoon. One-way despair. I had to occupy myself, I couldn't just wait for night. I needed a plan. So I made one, drank a whole bottle of red wine all by myself. Calmed me down. Hadn't eaten all day except some pistachio nuts after dancing class. I'll never stop dancing. Go and see my father in Connecticut, give M. time to think, me time to breathe, I'm always winded. Connecticut's too far, I'll go to the country. Call Saki and Chandrika. I want to go now. No one understands the immediacy of loneliness except the lonely. Look into renting a car. Maybe this Sunday.

Ten o'clock, chez *Marie Claire*: I arrive for a fitting, a job I thought confirmed, with four-month-old James hanging from my hand by his basket-bed handles. My first encounter with fashion since I was pregnant. All the editors are wearing black rectangular clothes. They encourage me, tap-slap me on the shoulder, kiss me on both cheeks, it's stifling hot and I'm sweating even more. They marvel over wriggling James and wish me luck. As if I'd come for tea. Show my baby to friends. Here's the veteran editor of the group, one of the ugliest women in the business, I only say that because I can't avoid seeing her, who stares at me and says in her shrill voice, suitably astonished:

'But, don't tell me you still *work*?' I stammer:

'No, yes, ah ... I think we're leaving for the States at the end of the year.' I lower my eyes to three seconds of silence. An eternity.

'But of *course* she still works.' Diplomatic Dora pipes up, cooing over James while a cigarette stub stays saliva-glued to a lower lip corner:

'*I'm* the one who asked for her.'

James, blinded by smoke and furious with my embarrassment, howls. I withdraw behind a desk and feed him. Other models arrive, show their portfolios, leave. I watch, ill at ease. Why am I surprised to find that nothing has changed? The editors are condescending and sacharine-sweet. The models look away while being stared at, swallowing their anger, desiring to please.

Finally I try on a rectangular black dress by Jean Louis Scherrer and leave.

Someone had called the agency by the time I got home, to cancel the job because I am too skinny.

June 20, 1983: Nine in the morning and already in Düsseldorf, – diapers rent money. First time I'm leaving James. I wish it was already over. Yet, I feel myself letting go, nerve-ends unwinding after months of idle worry at home. My life is not my own, today and tomorrow. I am between the gentle hands of the make-up man, (a short, muscular Turkish Bavarian, who took Tai-Chi night classes last year in San Francisco, paying for them by making and selling apfelstrudel during the day) and the monied hands of the slacks catalog client. In fact, the lack of anxiety when I work is such that I have to fight sleep. I'm falling asleep, I'm finally safe, on a down bed of German marks.

James, my baby man, mama's doing her best. Prince Charming's long gone.

Eleven a.m.: I'm naked. She's dressing me. Fat hands in flesh and gold run over my body without warning. Softly, glancing off, roughly, wrapping me. I jump and shrink and she starts again. I'd forgotten that there is nothing to feel. The slacks are badly cut, Fräulein, wrinkles are as normal as the Föhn wind. She scrutinizes, turns me in place, stands me up and still, she's crouched down, staring. If I move she springs to stop me, immobilizes me in a wrist grip, fumbles for a cigarette, lights and inhales desperately, smooths out my wrinkled sex.

A model is a model is a rose is a rose. Dreaming again. I'm here but I'm not. Someone raises my arm. I let it drop, a dead weight. Someone turns my head, looks at me quizzically. I smile back uncomprehendingly. Poor imbecile.

Twelve noon: Everything's going wrong. She shakes me. She must iron again.

'You are sweat-ting, matmoiselle . . .' – first time she's spoken to me. She thinks I'm French because I've been flown in from Paris. She's always thought like that.

I put a leg on the ironing board, offering my entire self. She doesn't think I'm funny. I laugh alone.

No one in Germany thinks I'm funny. Except in the dressing room, often, between the white wine and the sausages, to shake up the inherent inertia, to interrupt the obsessive inspection of angles in the mirror, to avoid another face mask recipe, to cut short the interminable list of best gynecologists, dermatologists, acupuncturists, homeopaths, laseropaths, Freudians, Jungians, Born Agains, tea leaf, tarot card, and aura readers, or to divert attention from the narration of another desperate love story, I bring out my folded paper of the first lines of dirty jokes, I remember the rest, and we become gratefully one, a chorus of manic shrieks and laughter.

Last year in this very same studio, the photographer threatened to send me home for unprofessionalism and provocation. Which surprised me because he's young, has hair to his shoulders, wears scruffy jeans, open-collared plaid flannel shirts, and plays oldies but goodies while we work. Laid back. Don't trust people's façades in fashion, except the alcoholics and schizophrenic girls. Our business is to make clothes look better than they are, and we osmotically carry that over to our persons, while giving the impression of not giving a shit. It's not true. We care.

One o'clock: She's ironing again. She's a pathological ironer, a common species of client. My waiting naked legs have goose bumps. The make-up man is also waiting quietly while I finish my sentence. It's funny how note-taking seems to inspire some sort of respect. Maybe that's why I do it . . . THERE SHE BLOWS! barges right into me, knocks the pen out of my hand, we have to step on it . . . stuff my shoulders, shoulder my tits, powder my blouse, iron my face, pin my skin, FILE MY TEETH! . . . FRÄULEIN GUNDLACH FOUND MURDERED: BITTEN TO DEATH.

The new model, a round blonde baby German, offering her face like a four-year-old to the Turkish Bavarian who gently blots her lips before she starts lunch. This is her first encounter with the almighty power of the make-up artist to render beautiful, a picture-perfect beauty she didn't know she had and won't ever, without him, and she's rightly awed.

Three o'clock: He's aiming for me agin, the make-up priest, approaching the no-seam paper, kleenex in the wind. What's the matter now? Ah yes. Cloth dolls don't sweat. I'll scour and scrub tonight. Buy one of each deodorant. I'm paid to be odorless, wrinkle-free and lumpless, nearly dimensionless, flat on the page.

Four o'clock: I can feel the nervousness, see the trying too hard of the baby German. The photographer talked to her, probably made her feel worse.

When I half open my mouth to look sexy in front of the camera, required more often than not, I feel instead my eyelids drooping and as if my jaw were about to dislocate. I'm so used to clenching it in place. Whereas I'm discovering after all these years that the two are not incompatible, clenching and relaxing. All you have to do is leave the lips parted while propeling them slightly forward, concentrating on the interior labial muscles, and instead of clenching the teeth, you flatten the middle of the tongue against the hard palate or roof of the mouth, thus creating the necessary tension, this last maneuver possessing the double advantage of accentuating the effect of voluptuousness as well as being a recommended exercise against double chins. All of which creates the spitting image of pre-orgasm and the camera gets carried away. How do other girls do it? Their faces are pulpier. I'm thin-lipped and pointy.

Make-up artists paint, models take pictures and/or go to acting school, photographers are working on a scenario and/or play the guitar, stylists are designing their own collections, editors keep diaries to be published. Everyone pretends to be something else, and we're all in it up to our necks, tepid water and quicksand.

You slowly become a moron as the day wears on. Everyone compares the number of hours they slept, hopes the hotel's not too desperate, thinks of calling home. The models make a date to eat early in the hotel restaurant, too tired and fed up to venture out. I dream of beer and sausages with horse radish, potato salad and apfelstrudel.

I miss James like a lover. I've known him for such a short time, have been modeling for so long, I start doubting the reality of my new life . . . James! Yes, my back hurts from holding you. How I wish I were holding you. I want to rush home and hug you hard against me.

I remember wanting to rush home to other arms, the old new loves, while sitting, stiff and pretty, silent and screaming, grateful playdough. It isn't any easier than it was.

Seven o'clock: Dinner in a Greek restaurant with the baby German. How did this happen? She'll be twenty-one tomorrow. Already pays herself a student lover, who, according to her needs, serves as agent, foil, chauffeur, handy-man or hit-man. I've known a few. She comes from a rich family, has always been spoiled. We had a heart-to-heart talk and I regret it as usual. There's an abyss between us. It's worse than talking to a pet, who at least gives you the impression he understands. She looks ill at ease. I don't blame her. I blame myself for so needing a listener, any pair of ears will do. It may be my worst habit.

June 21, five o'clock: Familiar crepuscular anxiety. Heart

racing, mind of its own. They've asked me to stay another day. I'll never get home.

From the very beginning you wait for the end. The last day is purgatory.

Six o'clock: Walking back to the hotel with the gentle make-up man, looking, as you don't look in the city you live in, at all the posters in the clean shop windows, advertising creams, cameras, camping equipment, beer – everyone is smiling the same smile, full of life, hysterical, empty-eyed. I disagreeably identify, feel my expression becoming theirs, my head turning into poster-size cardboard . . .

Bought a new German soap without soap for sensitive skins. One of the things I love about the traveling, and there are many though I've mentioned none and may not, is the international pharmacy it enables you to collect. Which pleasant thought prompts another: I am a mother and a citizen of the world.

Two star hotel. Someone's been bribed. Everything is low and cheap, from the touchable ceiling to the single chair. The orange-and-brown-flowered wallpaper echoes on the bedspread and hangs pathetically at the window, covering other curtains, in plastic, which hide the minute dimensions of the solitary window, which opens, finally, on to the turquoise wall of a prefabricated office building, so near that yesterday when I awakened at seven a.m., I excused myself to two German girls typing, who didn't seem to mind my naked body in their midst. There's no bathroom, only a shower, accessible by gliding in profile around the corner of a brown chipped formica table. Directing the shower knob against the far shower wall and bending my head sideways to meet the short slanting spray does not prevent the flood which every morning transforms about half the surface of the beige felt, uninflammable floor covering, peppered with cigarette burns, into a thin wet sponge. On the radio, invariably the same polka, the same as in the elevator, the restaurant, the lobby, and Düsseldorf airport.

June 22: Teutonic toucher's at it again, bull's-eye between the legs, whence comes all life and the worst wrinkles. And now the stylist with the beaten dog look and the quivering pupils, wonders what else she can do to justify her paycheck and make me unnaturally beautiful, her thankless daily task. She tries a red wooden bracelet, and another in braided gold, and a third, in royal-blue plastic and again, the silver-plated snake, the tortoiseshell rings, the charm bracelet of Swiss bells and Roman coins, all to hide my skinny wrists, unless, she shakes her head sadly, my arms are still too long for the jacket. Am I a replacement for a short husky blonde? She hands me falsies.

Left the same message on two answering services last night, M.'s and a forgettable one-night-stand's: 'From Düsseldorf with love.' Couldn't feel more alone.

Fräulein almost breaks my knee while turning my leg. I yell.

'Cum now, matmoiselle, I haf not hurt you. The pantz-in profeel, tso, iss bet-ter.' She football runs over to the photographer, pounces on the latest polaroid and spit-whispers into his ear. Everyone gets involved, hunches in a murmuring huddle. The sound amplifies, threatens. The studio is divided in two, jury and accused. I am guilty, I am guilty, I will pay for my sins just in case I've committed them. I may have.

I strike a new pose in profile and we continue.

Seven o'clock in the Düsseldorf airport: Feel so empty, don't even want to write it down . . . please . . . be there . . . wait for me . . . love me . . . no . . . listen, don't feel obliged.

Nine o'clock, Roissy: In general, I believe in pain as a valid agent of personal growth, but there are specific two minute intervals during which I would gladly exchange my heart for a ruthless painless model. Fuck him.

Paris, July 10, 1983, Sunday: Somewhere in between smoking cigarettes and sitting on the kitchen sink drinking beer, crying, and writing the latest in a series of letters to M., each one attempting to complete, rectify, and/or cancel out its predecessor, each one getting the best of me – mixing formula and changing James, watching his serious five-month-old-man's face and thinking, S., what the fuck are you doing? – I hear someone out the kitchen window whistling the opening march from the *Nutcracker Suite*, and realize how burdensome a broken heart is, because all of a sudden I feel weightless and happy, and astounded at the difference, and I cry again, relieved and sad that I certainly won't always be crying over M.

For as far back as I can remember, I used to sing in front of my house after dark – sing, hum, and whistle, dragging out the notes long and loud until I ran out of breath. Soprano high and bass low. Or comfortably loud in the middle and soft when a car went by. More often in the winter because it got dark early and was cold and people stayed inside. But they must have heard me. The whole street must have heard me but I felt deliciously alone. Sitting on the garbage cans in front of the curb. Like I owned the street.

I sing to James but he doesn't like it when my voice cracks. He prefers records. Charlie Parker. Mozart.

Inkster, Michigan, the fifties: I sang and danced for my parents in the kitchen because the linoleum was easy to turn on.

'Sue, you should be in musical comedy.' It was one thing they agreed on.

A group of five or six mothers from the neighborhood got together and put their little girls in the same dancing school so they could take turns driving us there and back. I was three years old. A few years later I was the only little girl still going. That was a thing about new suburbs. Not many kids did anything out of the ordinary, which means anything that was not eating, sleeping, going to school, church or watching television. Grown-ups bought new cars. Outside these primary activities it was an inert life-form. You fell off the end of the flat earth. Or were considered weird.

New suburbs were the first step out of the car factories in Detroit and the copper mines in upper Michigan. Many of our immigrant grandparents had spent the latter part of their lives being a lot less poor than in their native eastern Europe, but far from rich. Some of our fathers still worked in factories. Dancing lessons were as superfluous as champagne, which was reserved for wedding toasts, between the beer and the whiskey. You didn't become a professional dancer any more than you became a professional champagne drinker. Like a frilly party dress or Halloween costume you grew out of quickly, because you're growing so fast because you're eating so well. Eating was most important, eating lots. Finishing your piled-high plate. Appreciating it. Because as our parents told us often, *they* hadn't always had enough to fill their stomachs.

You took dancing lessons to be photographed on the front lawn in your tutu. After that, your father started complaining about the money, saying gym class was enough, especially after paying for the tutu.

So after everyone had had their picture taken, and were wearing their ballet slippers around the house, and gone back to watching Pinky Lee on Wednesday afternoons, I continued dancing until the age of twelve, having earned the right with my kitchen performances.

I learned classical ballet, tap-dancing, Chinese, Indian, and Hungarian folk dancing, vaudeville style (my teacher had been in vaudeville) French can-can, flapper dancing, and modern jazz. By the age of seven I could whistle the *Nutcracker Suite* by heart because our teacher used it for all our recitals. The 'Opening March' and 'Waltz of the Flowers' were performed every year, the *plats de resistance*. Plus it contains an Indian number, a Chinese number, and a Russian number which is Hungarian enough for new suburbs.

We gave our recitals, me and the other weirdos, in school gymnasiums, municipal auditoriums, a few times for hospitals, and even once for the U.S.O.*

I was eleven, we danced for a roomful of servicemen, wearing black leotards and fishnet stockings, black satin skirts

---

* Entertainment for U.S. service men overseas, (offices in every major U.S. city).

slit to the waist and black satin high heels. It was the first time I'd been dressed up like that, in what was for me 'Frederick's of Hollywood'. I used to gaze at their small box, eighth of a page advertisements, in the back of my mother's *Glamour*'s and *Mademoiselle*'s – the baby-doll nighties, the transparent peignoirs, the big breasts and rubber band waists and muscular thighs and calves of the women in the drawings. I wanted to look like that. I used to pretend I did when I masturbated with the paw of my giant stuffed dog every night. I didn't know what I was doing. I'd never heard the word for it. But I knew I was committing a mortal sin. And here I was on a stage, dressed practically like one of those advertisements. I was proud and almost convinced I was gorgeous but it was like wearing sex. Modern jazz movements are sexual. It was like asking for it. The servicemen were waiting for it. I could see it in their eyes, even if they were smiling like boy scouts. I could see it in their teeth, in their muscular jaws and necks, their beard stubble. I had never been so close to these concrete manifestations of the difference between me and them, the object of desire. I even avoided my father. Their heads were three feet away and below me, stage-lit – there. I went to Catholic school, to Mass every morning, in a thick, mid-calf, hunter-green skirt. I still hadn't given up the idea of becoming a nun. I said rosaries every day after school, alone in church, or at home, in front of my plaster statue of Our Lady of Perpetual Help and the altar of plastic flowers I'd arranged for her on top of my sock and underwear dresser. On my knees and so motionless I feared visions. The more my knees hurt, the longer I prolonged the pain, the more I wanted to itch and didn't, the more grace I accumulated, the higher my place in heaven.

I tried to do the entire number without opening my legs.

The teacher took me aside afterwards, said I was too young and a little too skinny, not to worry, I would change, but servicemen wanted to see girls with breasts. The more developed girls would continue the performances without me.

That same year we gave a recital for the mental patients in

Wayne State County Hospital. This time on stage with Tchaikovsky, in my tutu, moving everything but my ballet-tight hips with the strength of contained orgasms, I was excellent. They understand me, I thought. They need me. I love them.

I was even skinnier at twelve then at eleven and stopped going to dance class. Except once, with men's long underwear and four pairs of kneesocks under my pink tights. And breasts, a padded bra stuffed with kleenex. Mr Lawson, my teacher's husband, a thin balding giant who had to stoop in and out of doorways remarked, beaming at me: 'Susan's filling out!' Mrs Lawson gave her classes in the wood-panelled tile-floored basement of her home, and her often on welfare, ex-vaudeville magician husband was usually around. She had seen through my stuffed body and corrected her husband's optimistic appreciation, loudly – he wore a hearing aid – trying not to laugh. Mr Lawson looked at me, incredulous, then embarrassed, and maybe I imagined it, a little betrayed. I never went back.

I started taking records out of the public library and dancing alone in my basement every night. Forty-five minutes of warm-up followed by improvisation, to 'Bolero', 'The Rite of Spring', 'Swan Lake', 'Rhapsody in Blue', 'An American in Paris'. When I didn't recognize titles I'd choose records for the album cover or the lettering in the middle of the record. Discovering Ravel and Stravinsky alone in my basement was incredible. Sometimes I would crouch down and simply listen with the volume turned up. Sometimes I would thrash around to the point of occasionally falling, trying to live up to the music.

When I needed a public, I imagined servicemen spying through the basement windows. Or all my television heroes: Lassie's master, Rin Tin Tin's master, Fury's master, Soupy Sales, Raymond Burr, Richard Boone, Jeff Bridges, a few of the boys in the neighborhood, all the kids in my class at St Norbert's, and Mr Spengler, my handsome sandy-haired

English teacher and Korean war veteran. There was never a shortage. And it was just as well that I stopped going on my own. My father left that year and there was no more money for classes.

It never entered my mind.
'You didn't help me,' my mother said.
I'm sorry, it never entered my mind. I knew you weren't happy. It was painful to know. And embarrassing. I thought maybe you were just like that. How could I have helped? I was in a shell. Is that the guilt? That it didn't even enter my mind. It still feels bad. But you never explained. You never told me much. I didn't even know if you loved him. I still don't know. You fought so violently. For so many years. Then you were stoic. You shouldn't have been. Or were you disabled by what you couldn't have been prepared for? In fact I never thought much about my mother. We were a small family of needy inept strangers. I never helped her. But she never told me she needed help. We screamed at each other. She slapped me. I slapped her back.

'You'll *never* get along with *anyone*! You think it's any different later on? Getting along begins in the home. You can't get along with me, you'll *never* get along with *anyone*!' I must have hurt her. I'm sure she didn't want to hurt me. I can't even remember.

She had her nose done twice. It was my father's idea. He took me to visit her in Straith Memorial Hospital, downtown Detroit. There were two rows of large color photographs in the hallway outside my mother's room, brightly lit from behind, before and after shots. Bulbous growths on noses and necks, well enough focused to see the contents of pores.

She was black and purple and yellow and swollen and bandaged, as if she'd been beaten badly. Why did she let him? I was afraid to get too near her in the bed, to really see her face. She was like the before photographs. I was twelve, everything happened when I was twelve. By the time she was operated on again, my father had left.

One night he called from New Jersey and told her he wanted a divorce. Long conversation. You answered in murmurs and short sentences. I listened, afraid to hear and not to hear. You brought me on to the couch afterwards and softly announced it. I wasn't expecting it. Everything was wrong but I thought it was finally going to be right. I thought we were going to move there. He was supposed to be finding a house. He'd already been gone for two years but we were always on the point of joining him. You needed comfort that night. I was sad and numb. You kept insisting it wasn't our fault, mine or my brother Jimmy's. Kept insisting. Jimmy wasn't home. You told him later and I heard it all twice. I wished you would stop talking. Anyway, he'd already left.

It was a rainy Saturday afternoon. He came and got us, me and Jimmy, instead of just calling out our names. Brought us into the living room and sat us down at his feet. He sat in the dark brown easy chair next to the front door. It had a fringe along the bottom I used to run my fingers through. The carpet was strewn with last Sunday's comics, making sloppy tents. While he spoke, I kept trying to make out the print in the balloons of L'il Abner. He cried the first, then left with two big suitcases.

On Sunday I awakened early and peeked in on my mother, not really expecting to see her alone. It was the first time he hadn't come home all night. I went and leaned on the frame of my bed feeling as rigid as the wood. I dug my nails into my palms, my fists into my eyes, trying to lessen the hurt with another. It was worse than the nausea before throwing up.

My mother took us for a drive in the afternoon. It was raining again but she drove even slower than the rain called for, like a snail, slowing down long before red lights, and hesitating before starting up again when they turned green. We were silent in the car. Except she told us not to tell anyone, our friends or the neighbors. That it wasn't any of their business. If anyone asked where he was, to say he was on a trip. I think she was waiting for him to come home. She, like me, didn't quite believe he'd gone yet.

And he came back. First on short visits, then to stay. Then he left again. Once after a short visit, Christmas or Easter, we were on our way to drop him off somewhere in the car, a slow song came on the radio:

'Daddy's home . . . Daddy's home . . . to stay.'

'That's just what we need, huh?' my father said, and changed the station.

This leaving was final. Something to be understood but not dwelled upon. Dirty Dad. Dirty other woman. He never mentioned her but I knew she must exist. Dirty clothes in the back seat. Did he think I was blind? I always pretended I hadn't seen them. They were often there.

I didn't hate. I didn't love. Love and hate were just as unsatisfactory, equally impossible. I was half one and half the other and couldn't stand it.

When I was six years old, sitting in the freshly-mown grass, smelling it, listening to the bees, the crickets, the sun burned but was never too hot. In the sand I liked getting dirty. In the snow I didn't mind getting wet. I liked being hot and cold. Life was sensual and reassuring.

I used to wait for daddy to come home, wait in the driveway for his car to pull up. I always had something important to tell him. He'd pick me up, even when I started getting too big, kiss me on the head and carry me into the house.

'How's my Susie-woosie?' He didn't really listen to what I said but it didn't matter.

We went swimming in the summer and sledding in the winter. I loved being frightened of the cold waves in Dearborn Lake, the icy hills in Inkster Park. Daddy frightened me and laughed harder than I did.

He took me to see Jerry Lewis movies. We laughed harder than anyone in the cinema. People would turn and stare at us.

He tickled me until I could hardly breathe.

Every night I'd listen to the train passing behind Michigan Avenue, about a mile and a half from our house. I imagined myself on the train and was glad to be in my dark, safe bed. I could be in both places at once. I could travel anywhere. A boy kept kissing me as I fell asleep. The train whistle, long and lonely, insistent, made the kissing more exciting.

Paris, July 11, 1983: I feel at home in neighborhood cafés, half falling apart and dirty, crowded, where I'm anonymous, full of artisans and immigrants, retired people, people on welfare, and drunks, the truth and lying of alcohol, the seeking help that makes people drink and dream.

I like this one, the Brady, on the Faubourg St Denis near dancing class. It has a windowed side wall in the back with the tables, with a view on to an arched passageway. On the other side of the passage is a bedroom furniture store, Yvon's, cluttered with fifties and sixties style mattresses and bedsteads which look half mummified. Thick straight lines or heavily carved curlicues. And bed-table lamps which are thin rods of in-curving dusty gold metal with kitsch, tulip-shaped metal shades. It's like gazing into the parent's bedroom of a childhood girlfriend, ominous, smelling of stale or mothballs. The longer I sit the more forbidden I feel so I sit for five minutes more, enjoying it, and the slight high of a beer on an empty stomach, seeking help and dreaming, smoking, negating the healthy effects of the dancing class I've just taken, wishing someone would come up and start screaming at me about wasting time so I could scream back – that I need this, to leave me alone, and to thank them for taking the trouble. And perhaps offer to buy them a drink.

The masculine, sunburnt-faced girl cripple always sits on the ground at different places along the Faubourg St Denis, summer and winter. Her stockinged crippled feet on a square of old carpeting, a tin bowl between her legs bent up at the knees. She watches passers-by and talks back to whomever talks to her with rough camaraderie. I wince every time I pass her. She is about my age. She makes me angry. They all make me angry. I can't bring myself to give her a few francs. Acknowledging the pity I don't want to feel. The insulting reminder to her that I am not a cripple. Of course I'm not.

I want to sit down beside her and talk as to a sister but I don't have the courage. I want to tell her a story of a beauty and a beast but that would be grotesque.

I've never dared to live except in my model's face. Is it so boringly simple as that? I lived quite well at times. And everyone needs a façade. I laughed more than I did anything else all those years, except maybe change clothes, and I'm laughing more and more; I could become a professional laugher. But I've also become impatient, aggressive, unoccupied. Stuck in the streets with the crumbs of the model face and nowhere to go but home to daddy. He said he'd be happy to take care of me and James for the time it takes me to readjust. Thank you daddy. But I loathe the idea of being taken care of. People have been taking care of me for thirty-three years. And what is readjust? Putting my legs in the place of my arms, my arms in the place of my legs and learning to walk? I already know how to walk like that.

Daddy, have I pleased you now? Are you proud of your model daughter? It was your idea.

> A modeling career sounds like the moon when you come from a
> blue-collar suburb of Detroit, and your grandparents speak
> with a Croatian accent, and boys don't like you because you're
> skinny and clumsy, a stilt-bird with acne bowing shyly towards
> the heads of her classmates. You feel great sitting down when
> everyone else is standing.
> 'Seduce a Top Model' – French *Vogue* for men.

Detroit, 1961: My father signs me up for a subteen modeling

contest in J L Hudson's department store. I refuse to stand next to him while he fills in the form in case a shopper strolling by realizes what he is doing and think *I* have requested it, that *I* think I'm pretty enough to be a model. He proceeds to choose my outfit for the audition and I half-heartedly accompany him, agreeing to everything even if I think it's awful: a turquoise and white checked, full-skirted shirtwaist dress, a yellow straw inverted bowl which is supposed to be a hat and which I particularly hate (my father says it makes me look like Grace Kelly, I'm always Grace Kelly for my father), and white satin flats which will be dyed the same rare yellow as the hat at great expense.

Mom is furious about the money.

I write a commentary and recite it, describe my outfit as if I'm selling it, into a microphone on an enormous stage, in an enormous auditorium, two weeks later, while the straw bowl rides up and almost off my head because it's too small.

I have an involuntary orgasm while waiting my turn, which I try to hold back so it comes even quicker; I'm sure everyone knows. Thinking about it afterwards is a secret pleasure I don't quite feel bad about.

I start wearing the four pairs of kneesocks, men's long underwear, black opaque tights and stuffed padded bra to school every day. I don't want my mother to suspect my 'secret'; she'll ask questions if I do a load of wash every night. So my feet smell by the end of the week. And hurt when I stand too long or walk because all the socks make my shoes too small. But I can't ask for bigger ones. That too would be suspicious and my feet are already giant size nine's. All of which make my calves the right size but my ankles a bit thick.

I win the contest in flesh-colored hose. I have to put them back on every other Saturday. Take off my comforting calves and admit my calfless chopsticks to a crowd of inquisitorial strangers during a half-hour subteen fashion show. I keep the bra on. It's obligatory. Sometimes I take the kleenex out, but in or out I move as stiffly, to prevent the cup seams folding up and in, or the kleenex moving around too much like up to my shoulder blades and down to the ground, while I follow its trajectory, turning purple.

I reel out of the dressing room and up the four steps, walk and back, walk and back and turn, seek the woman commentator's eyes every time I stumble off the podium for confirmation that I look as dizzy up there as I feel. She smiles at me reassuringly every single time.

I'm proud of having won. To be able to wear all those beautiful clothes as if they were mine, even if it's only for half an hour.

I wander around the store aisles after the show, wanting one of everything. You could buy a new life if you had the money. I steal my mother's charge card every once in a while for a skirt or a pair of shoes, knowing she won't get the bill for a month. Then she screams and hides the charge card, but I always find it.

Paris, July 12, 1983: Fashion show for Le Printemps. The girls here are either very normal girls with whom the public can immediately identify and even wonder how *she* got to be a model, or faded beauties like myself. That's what happens – hometown department stores, to New York, Paris, Milan, Tokyo, covers of *Vogue*, divinity among the fashionable élite, ideal for star worshippers – and back to department stores. I've bought most of my make-up here for fifteen years. Le Printemps is next to my agency Paris Planning's old office on the rue Tronchet. Being a salesgirl, of sorts, today, instead of a rich shopper; this is really the end of my brilliant career. In front of a large crowd of inquisitorial strangers.

I bought a money belt on the main floor before rehearsal time. And three leotards I don't need and can't afford. Am amazed at the psychological implications of what I buy. Money, to dance. As well as being a re-enactment of my stolen charge-card purchases, spending money that is not mine but I think I deserve, a compensation that feels like necessity. So he was right. The psychoanalyst before last told me – I'm a banal case of hysterical adolescent narcissism. I wish he had only suggested it.

Inkster, Michigan, 1962–63: I don't talk about the modeling at St Norbert's. I don't think anyone will believe me. My new thick legs don't go unnoticed, especially in the spring when I finally take off the long underwear and black tights because I'm sweating so much, and wear only the four pairs of kneesocks. The outer pair often slip down, revealing a strip of red or blue underneath. Sometimes I hear giggling behind me while the class is filing back from Mass in the morning. Without looking back, I reach down and pull the green ones back up over the other three pairs.

The boy I secretly like is pleased with the weight I'm gaining. Like Mr Lawson. They see what I want to show them. Maybe you just have to be careful not to show them anything else.

My friends avoid me this year. I often end up walking home behind Karen and Patricia. They walk slowly, touching sides; I end up practically on top of them because you walk faster when you're alone. But I never pass them, give them a chance to laugh at me behind my back, even if I'm dying of impatience. I start muttering loud enough for them to hear, about how they're so stuck up they don't even think their own shit stinks, as a boy I like said to me once. They turn and snicker, turn away and draw closer, leaning on each other.

I have one friend, red-haired freckle-faced Claudia, who asked me once why I wore all that and then answered for me:

'You must be cold. Are you cold?'

'Yes.'

Claudia's father works in a factory; she has five brothers and sisters. Her parents manage to send most of them to St Norbert's but can't afford to buy them nice clothes. Claudia makes her own. She can make difficult things like pleated skirts and ruffled blouses. She is outspoken, mature for her age, at ease with adults. The kids at school are afraid of her. She protects me. We steal together and never get caught. I'm grateful for and jealous of her friendship but her courage frightens me too.

She coaxes me into running away with her on a girl scout camp weekend. We walk in the woods all morning, photographing each other posing on logs. Then we find the nearest town and get caught before you can say 'jack rabbit jump'. The camp director is stopped at a red light in a station wagon as we walk out of the woods at the same intersection. She opens the car door and orders us to 'get in!' in a voice of almighty wrath determined to murder us if necessary, before the rape and murder headlines holding her responsible hit the newsstands. I am stricken mute and immobile, but at least now I won't have to meekly follow my friend if she decides we should hitchhike to New York. Claudia doesn't seem to mind getting caught, although I'm sure she'd prefer hitchhiking to New York. She's fearless.

We were to be detained in the camp dormitory for the rest of the weekend, but Claudia talked the director into letting us off after half an hour. She gets as much as she can out of any given situation, and invariably more than the person wants to give, child or adult, friend or enemy. She's afraid of dogs. You can't reason with them. I'm always behind her, vacillating between fear and freedom, never opening my mouth until we're alone. The most I can manage in the vicinity of an adult, outside a disciplined classroom, is trying so hard to understand everything he or she is saying that I often don't.

The show tomorrow will take place in the sixth floor restaurant under a startling stained glass dome. Le Printemps was founded in 1865, and blessed by the parish priest of the Madeleine. Which didn't prevent the store from burning to the ground in 1881. It was reconstructed the same year by Paul Sedille, and because of the latter's extensive and innovative use of ironwork, for decoration as well as armature, the new

Printemps was considered the most modern department store of its time.

One of the advantages of the end of a modeling career is the ever more pressing desire to replace it with any kind of knowledge. I ask questions now I would never have asked before. I demand food for thought – good food, fast food, any food – which will permit me to momentarily leap out of the skin of someone I'm slowly defining as a nearly autistic child, when she isn't an aging dancing bear.

Maeva, my Vietnamese friend, arrives. Announces she has signed with the same record producer as Grace Jones. Complains of jealousies, people being mean when things start to work out. Making lots of money modeling is never considered, among models, as enough. We want to sing, dance, get into the movies, marry Mick Jagger.

I'm dreaming. Someone is playing the *Köln Concert*. I look up from my book and see a panama-hatted fat man in a white suit, sunglasses and a beard, trying out a piano on the stage. I guess he'll be playing for us tomorrow. I will thank him personally for being here and saving us from the ritual disco sex-stride cassette. I can't listen to my *Köln Concert* album at home without doing the dishes. Or I listen to side one, then feel obliged to go out and do the shopping. I really appreciate it when I'm 'forced' to enjoy because it's part of the job, and I don't have to feel guilty for not dusting the tables or performing some other small penance at the same time. For the moment I'm being paid to wait. It's like some heavenly benevolent force rewarding me with a short state of grace, pouring glitter on my good girl's head for trying so hard, to stay alert, not miss one single duty of a guilty single working mother and ex-super-party-model who spent all her cash in restaurants and discotheques, buying people's love, and now she's got shit-all for her own flesh and blood, and can't keep a man because the bottomless pit of her whiny needs scares him away. Facts, S. Don't be afraid. And be as subjective as you damn well please. It's every woman's privilege.

I let myself read on jobs, sometimes even at home but that's different. That's bettering myself. Models often suffer from inferiority complexes and read only 'good' books. I carried *Ulysses* around in my make-up bag during three different six-month periods. If I managed to take the book out of the bag, in the middle of analyzing world events with the hairdresser and stylist, read a paragraph and understand a sentence, I was happy for the rest of the day. I was a thinking person who just happened to be a model in her free time.

I feel doubly fortunate today, reading *Madame Bovary* to Keith Jarrett. And James giggled at me this morning, several times, his whole body giggled, he sounded like a well-mannered forty-year-old. I was making faces at him. The subtlest change in an expression made him explode in giggles again, which makes me think he must have a very sophisticated sense of humor and in any case is a terrific audience. The sun is shining, even if I can't see it from inside the department store. My health is fine, except for my nerves. My cup runneth over instead of the usual half empty.

I have to move my car and they're treating me like a big girl, letting me go alone. Second dream for the day: let loose in a darkened department store after closing time. One of the advantages of a modeling career *before* the end is the right to be in places (museums, theatres, restaurants, factories, department stores) at odd times. It's easy to isolate yourself from the group, and be alone surrounded by mankind's accomplishments and prior existence; today's or twenty or a thousand years ago's. An historical voyeuse. It excites me sexually.

I should steal something. I'm right next to the discount shampoo section. I wouldn't get caught unless a guard happens to be watching on a surveillance screen. He's not expecting anyone. (They wouldn't have called down to warn of my arrival?) And I've been watched for years. But not stealing. I'd simply hand it back to him. Throw it at him and run. Maybe I should dance. Undress slowly. Maybe he'd leave his spy station hiding place and join me, grab me. Maybe he'd stay where he was and undress slowly while watching me on television . . . I'm demented . . . then again . . . Claudia could saunter up and down the aisles being very selective, taking as much as her bag and pockets could hold.

If he's there he must be wondering why I've been standing still for five minutes. Enjoying the Big Brother relationship and trying to be brave. Except I'm not. A giant bottle of discount shampoo doesn't seem worth it and I'm not Claudia, nor an exhibitionist. Unconvinced, I walk out past a good-looking guard in a small windowed room watching Benny Hill on a regular television, who is as startled by my sudden appearance as if I'd walked past him naked, and as I am by his.

The streets are as empty as inside the store, except for a paralyzed man being wheeled home by a friend, a hot chestnut stand attached to his wheelchair. I walk slowly behind them, wondering where they're going, watching them think they're alone, relishing the emptiness where there's usually a crowd, pleasantly blinded by the sun going down at the end of Boulevard Haussmann, and disappointed in myself for not even stealing the shampoo.

Find an alcove to eat in during rehearsal break, big bay windows on to Parisian roofs on three sides. The sky is blue-black now, the sun radiant dark yellow, warming my alcove and my back like the body of a lover. In fact what I really like is being alone with something specific to do shortly afterwards, even if it's something stupid. It's like I need a 'think break' after each step I take, to realize where I am and the numerous other places I could be, because I can't seem to think and step at the same time. I've always been uncoordinated, but to say I'm overly conscious of it lately would be an understatement.

An old chandelier is hanging from the ceiling in my alcove, art-deco dirty gold metal and frayed wires, ready to fall on someone's head, mine of course. This beautiful space has been recently redecorated, part-fast food, part-English pub. The tables and chairs are orange and white plastic, indifferent round-edge assembly-line puzzle pieces in the same two forms.

The floor is covered in two shades of worn-out red and black wool flowers, smelling of stale industrial food, feet and beer.

One floor down in the building across the street, three plaster mannequins in nurse's uniforms are leaning against each other and the glass pane with vacant expressions. I'd knock on the window and wave if I wasn't a little afraid they'd wave back. I wish rehearsal break was longer. I wish I didn't feel like avoiding the people I work with.

Bongos have arrived and they are jamming. Soul Food (like the sunlight). Thank God the Muzak's off. If the Muzak was on I'd take a valium, put my fingers in my ears and hiss until it worked. I'm sure there are no statistics, but I wonder how many fragile temperaments and tired business travellers have haywired the five hundredth time they heard the theme song from *Dr Zhivago* or *Love Story*?

The clothes we'll be wearing are as shapeless as the new furniture. The real music, real sky, the stained glass dome, are all the more remarkable for surrounding ugliness.

One of my 'numbers': white, heart-shaped sunglasses with red polka-dots, too small for me. A red nylon jersey suit with white polka-dots, too big for me. A white gauze bandana, red polka-dots. Beige, stretch net gloves, that start out the size of a premature baby's hand and take three minutes to get on.

The whole shebang will last a quarter hour. More than enough time for the public to get the idea. What idea?

There is something wonderful about going out on to a fashion show podium with a strange man's arm around you, even if you know he's getting paid to do it, you forget, and something horribly corny, not even insulting, when he doesn't pay any attention to you except as an accessory to *his* passage. I'm drunk on two beers. Don't they even turn the heat off in these places?

Rat's hole to dress in, as usual. The escalator is right in back of its improvised burlap wall. Lean against the thumbtacked fabric hiding our nakedness, thinking it solid, you fall down the moving stairs. Forty-five square feet for fifteen people.

I'm dressing next to the black bombshell who did Louis de Funes's last movie. I think she thinks she's still doing it, and that this is her private dressing room, and that all the other people are easy chairs and flower vases and couches installed for her pleasure and comfort. Being the closest couch at hand, I receive the fall of her graceful heavy arm the most often. She's only nice to the male model who is an accessory to most of her passages in the show.

She complains about being kept waiting for the last run-through:

'I'm working early tomorrow . . .' she says three times but never within hearing of anyone with authority. Maybe her intention was to let the four models sitting nearby know she was in demand.

'O.K., I'm telling them we have to start now . . .' and she doesn't move, stays seated on her puzzle piece straight as a rod, more virtuous than my French ex-mother-in-law. Black lady with thick pursed lips.

She takes up the whole horizontal length of the mirror in the dressing room, stretching her arms into her fur coat and her hand into my face. It's eighty degrees today. Does she have to look at herself to understand what she's doing? I wish I could look into a mirror and know.

July 13, Show Time: It is *hot*. A *long* speech is being given, by a government minister. I'm not listening and I'm sure everyone is bored silly. Something about how France can be proud of its cultivated couture. All these terrible clothes are French. The show will include the 'Queen of Sheba', token black model from Guadaloupe, France-Outre-Mer, and budded film star; and two black American dancers who will boogie around in Printemps underwear. Don't white people wear underwear? Don't black people wear clothes? The Queen of Sheba does, but she's like the rest of us, cellulite on her gorgeous thighs. And I'll bet she can't boogie.

The buffet is sumptuous: whiskies, wines, fruit juices, champagne in ornate silver pails, expensive-tasting canapés, exotic fruits, six-foot-high flower arrangements, and trees. I guess that didn't leave any money for chairs. The jungle is surrounding the audience on three sides. The stage is on the fourth. The space in the middle is too small for six hundred people. No one is eating or drinking, or has the right to, did anyone ask? I did, and was refused. The models are waiting in their rat hole, dresssed and sweating. I wonder how a tired thirsty crowd will endure watching the show, imprisoned in an inaccessible garden of gluttonous delights.

Finally the minister finishes his speech and opens the bar. The models wait and sweat a half hour more while the crowd gets pissed.

There had been a pleasant moment earlier when the panama-hatted piano player asked for three whiskies for the musicians and was given a bottle. I was one of the musicians. I lost track of the time and had to be paged urgently, was bawled out upon my arrival in the rat hole, and had a short fight with my dresser. Whiskey makes me mean. She grabbed my clothes and threw them into a messy corner. I grabbed them back and took my time.

The show goes over my head. All I remember is being annoyed and feeling slightly triumphant on the podium, wearing children's polka-dot sunglasses, five feet above a plebeian public.

Talk with a friend afterwards, a press agent with granny glasses, small, plump, lovable, who puts two papaya into my bag for James. He tells me I should keep modeling, that there were only three or four girls like me, that had made such an impact, that it didn't matter that I wasn't doing much important work anymore; the image would never die. Sweet man. He loves his images and doesn't like to see them hit the dust. He was sure I could go on forever. I explain:

'*Fuck* the impact! *What* impact? The image is exactly what I want to get away from! And I'm almost thirty-four for Christ's sake, it's getting rid of *me*!'

I drive him home. He tells me he lives in the middle of fashion magazines, that he needs them, that he surrounds himself with 'chiffons', bolt ends of luxurious fabric. That he needs to 'play dolls'. That maybe he was sick, women couldn't stand it. His wife had left him because he was always dressing her up and then changing his mind. That he was always changing his women's clothes and they inevitably left him. Poor left Teddy Bear and Barbie Doll. Mine leave me too.

He suggests I start a line of clothes.

'But I'm not Cheryl Tiegs or Christy Brinkly!' I shout.

'O.K.,' I continue, 'bright yellow two-and-a-half-inch platforms, purple crushed velvet A-line granny dresses, with puff sleeves and patchwork lace-up bodices. And the velvet changes color when you change directions. I had a dress like that.' He laughs uneasily.

'I'm serious! The late sixties, second degree! . . . only *you* do it.' He's hurt and I feel terrible.

'I'm sorry! But hearing you talk like that is like having to listen to the theme song from *Dr Zhivago* on a plane. It's moving music but it drives me nuts! But I'm flattered! I'm really flattered and it drives me nuts . . .'

My father leaves the year I model for Hudson's. He comes to pick me up every other Saturday before the show, takes me to the hairdresser's, drives me downtown, and goes back to wherever he lives. Always a different hairdresser, so no one gets familiar, starts asking questions:

'Oh, so you guys live in Inkster? So what are you and your dad doing way out here?'

'Oh, my dad doesn't want to bump into any of our neighbors.'

Once he takes me to a hairdresser who gives me a flat on top pageboy, no teasing. Teased hair and the padded bra were all I had left after taking off my stuffed legs. I feel defenseless and avoid looking in the mirror. My father and the woman keep saying, one after the other, that I look so much more my age, so much prettier:

'... without all that ratting and hairspray for grown-ups.' It was as if they'd planned my hair-do together before I got there. The woman compliments the quality of my hair.

'Like your father's. You shouldn't hide it in a bunch of knots.' I start crying as soon as we get out the door of the salon, and tease my hair in the car during the ride downtown.

Two years later, and the first summer I spend in New Jersey, my father comes to get me and Jimmy and drives us to a motel to pick up his new wife, the flat-on-top-pageboy-hairdresser, whom he obviously doesn't remember I've already met. So his recent request for a divorce didn't mean he'd met his new wife recently. Here was tangible proof of a fact my adolescent mind had only menaced itself with; I play deaf and dumb for most of the summer.

They'd bought a ranch home on credit, in a new pseudo-upper-class district near Princeton. There's a lot of space, so Jimmy and I both get our own thin-walled room. The doors echo all over the house when you close them, so I close my door slowly and spend most of the summer reading on the floor, forgetting where I am.

I read *The Group* by Mary McCarthy, in which I learn that thin girls are more sensual because their nerve-endings are closer to the surface; and that it's rare for women to have orgasms the first time they make love. And that there are two kinds of homosexual, those who admit it and those who don't. I look up homosexual in the dictionary but not sodomy; it sounds biblical, and forget what I don't really understand. Not until years later, when I start modeling and being intimidated by one beautiful unresponsive man after another, do I finally figure out, with a sense of exclusion, the meaning of the word.

I figure out what an orgasm is. I also read the *New York Times Review of Books* cover to cover. I have to really concentrate to understand it and am proud when I think I do. I read Nabokov because he is praised so highly: *Pnin*, and *The Real Life of Sebastian Knight*; both of which I find in the Princeton Public Library. I realize, this time, that the content is beyond me, but I don't mind. Mary McCarthy's facts of life, which I had so happily half understood, pale in the face of my infatuation with Nabokov. His litanies of onomatopeas, his 'metaphysical' sense of suspense, his whole new magical world, makes me as happy as I have ever been. I figure that fourteen-year-olds don't usually read him and feel like a proud initiate, like all of a sudden I have an edge over everyone my own age, in fact over everyone who has never read Nabokov, which is everyone I know. And I had found him all by myself (including *Lolita*, on the bus into Princeton one day), chosen him from among dozens of authors reviewed in the *New York Times*. I have to talk about my great discovery. My father works all day, my little brother Jimmy will never understand and anyway, he'd left, back to Michigan to keep my mother company. I was alone all day with the hairdresser. So that's how we start talking, about Nabokov. I talk and she listens.

Then we start playing poker in the evenings with my father. I am no longer the daughter, I am a person, who reads better books than they do. They are no longer the father and the father's wife, they are two other people, Bob and Maureen, and we get along like any regular set of card-playing buddies.

When I'm not reading or talking or playing cards or eating or sleeping, I masturbate.

Back in Michigan, I discover a psychology book of my mother's hidden under the couch (and *Lolita* hidden in a drawer), which explains masturbation as a normal healthy phenomenon. It's been a summer of discoveries.

Cherry Hill High, mid-sixties: Joy Ann, tagging after me, jelly-jowled Joy Ann. Please go away, please don't sidle up to me like that.

I walk down hallways with my books hugged against my breasts to hide their absence and my shoulders hunched, as if banded like a mummy to the waist, branching out in pear-shaped loose-muscled skinniness.

My heart pounds wildly fifty yards away from someone I should greet, and often, awkwardly, pretend not to see. I study because I'm lonely, and fall in love with my teachers, listening with hungry eyes, joy of learning, imagining other joys. I'm attractive prey for other misfits, the class zombie, there's always one, I hope I'm not another. A girl, a boy, who is shy, tall, skinny and gangly, or short, chubby, and graceless, who moves left when everyone else moves right, whose arms and legs don't seem properly attached.

Joy Ann is six feet tall, flat-chested, masculine, mustached, a nice body which doesn't make up for the rest. You notice that her limbs seem rubbery, to bend in the wrong places, and that she smells like greasy hair and a dirty house. She acts like she has a lot of self-confidence. She often looks on the verge of doing something important, she's often hurrying. And when she's not hurrying she's shuffling, duck-toed, and talking to herself. She has fish eyes and crew-cropped hair, which make her look like an asylum escapee or a defrocked nun. And because we both work half days in the same library, she's latched on to me, keeps inviting me to her house. I never go. I change hallways when I see her coming. People might think we're friends.

I wonder what will become of her? How will she insert herself into society? She has an older sister, as self-confident as herself, who joined the army. Maybe Joy Ann will follow in her sister's footsteps.

Maybe she'll become a model. She's six feet tall and has a nice body and you never know – a shampoo and a haircut, a few dancing lessons . . .

New Jersey, Summer '66: 'Isn't it a shame? Susan never filled out . . .' my father must have lamented to his new wife. I wonder if my flat chest embarrassed him. I wonder when he stopped waiting for it to grow.

'She may be a late bloomer, you just wait. In a few years, she'll be a gorgeous girl. She may be a gorgeous girl.' He'd been saying things like that for a while. I'd been so pretty till puberty, he couldn't admit I might end up banal, and chestless.

He stares at my chest every time I arrive for the lonely New Jersey summer. I start wearing baggy clothes.

His wife has enormous tits. It'd been the first thing I'd noticed after recognizing her coming out of the motel. (Why did it have to be a motel? Why couldn't it have been someone's normal house?)

The third summer I spend with them I work as a waitress in the Ranch Room restaurant in the Princeton shopping center. One of the other waitresses is seven months pregnant and has a factory worker husband who comes to pick her up every afternoon. He walks in in his black leather greaser jacket and a slow swagger, already cracking jokes. She serves him coffee in the back while he waits for her to finish her shift. People go and sit with him because he's so funny, a real card, which is about the best thing to be in America after rich and righteous. And he never laughs at his own jokes. He stares laughter out of his audience with an expectant deadpan. I listened in joy, horror, and incomprehension, the day he said he was waiting impatiently for his wife to lay the egg because he was tired of climbing mountains.

He says I'm sexy in my glasses and white uniform. I'm a little afraid he's making fun of me. I've been told, not often, that I'm beautiful, but no one has ever called me sexy. Being associated with the subject that almost exclusively occupies your thoughts is like being given the right to think about it, even to practice it, even without tits. And it sounds authoritative out of the mouth of a greaser in a black leather jacket. The greasers at school ignore me. And I look down on them because I figure they're good for nothing, that they'll all end up in prison. But they're sexy. And maybe they're not all bad.

With the money I make I take ballet lessons every day after work. My father comes to pick me up sometimes, watches the end of class. Says he thought I'd dance better than that after all those years of classes.

Paris, July 28, 1983: Tired, tired. A heat wave. Chanel show later on in the Beaux Arts School. James talked to his stuffed dog for an hour this morning. Mlle Marie, from Kid's Service (an extravagantly expensive babysitting service), says he's advanced for his age.

Quai Malaquais: Four make-up artists, seven models, fifteen hairdressers and two miscellaneous (I counted) in a room minute even before the tables for blow-dryers, make-up installations, bobby pin boxes, and a mountain of hot hairpieces, were installed. Two of the hairdressers are working. One has just started on me; the other thirteen are getting a bun lesson from M Alexandre, who comments as his protégé Daniel twists complicated hairpiece loops on to Felicitas's bowing nape. My friend Anne Marie keeps muttering:

'There are thirty people in this room . . . What are they all doing here? . . . Aren't they supposed to know how to make a bun?' She flops down next to me and says wearily:

'Fire in the house.'

The aristocratic bacheloress I met on a formal hunting weekend with my aristocratic ex-before-last, who pretends she doesn't know me 'on the job' (she's some sort of press agent; I've never understood the different sorts), is doing her lifted face with bits and pieces off the make-up table. Competing rather successfully in our cubicle, she pushes people in the small of the back with two dry knuckles and says 'par*don*' without looking at them; never losing sight of the blusher or pencil she wants, and grabs.

M Alexandre stops his teaching and drops his comb, scurrying off to usher Jerry Hall to someone else's comfortable seat. She has arrived as colorfully made up as a full crayon box, accompanied by her baby daughter and the nurse. The more the merrier. The master begins, he's been saving himself, assisted by three apprentices, a quarter of the blondy locks each. The four of them back up about a yard, brushing the golden wheatfield to its horizontal length. The only space left in the room is underneath Jerry's hair.

I remember when she started and watching her rise, inventing compliments for everyone along her path paved with men and dresses, including me. Once we ended up next to each other during a Valentino show *bis*, bowing, crouching, taking porcelain figurine positions in full-skirted ball gowns straight out of *War and Peace*. She lifted up her skirt and fluffed it out on both sides, thus crushing and covering mine. My blood rose. I was hurt. She'd told me I looked like Vanessa Redgrave. I fluffed my skirt over hers. And she fluffed her skirt over mine. And I fluffed my skirt over hers. She finally backed down. I would have gone on forever. She'd started it.

The security guard is explaining to peach-skinned New York model Peggy B., with obvious pleasure, the various contents of the catered sandwiches – leaning in close and pointing:

'Jam-*bon* . . . pâ-té-de-lé-*gumes* . . .' enunciating slowly because Peggy doesn't understand French. I watch from the small noisy terrace overlooking the quay, where everyone takes momentary refuge from the suffocating heat inside. Peggy sees me watching and joins me on the other end of the terrace. We small-talk about babies. She reaches inside her bag, extracts her personal brown bread wrapped in paper toweling (I wonder if she brought it from America?) and delicately constructs a messy sandwich with the vegetable pâté, throwing the offensive *brioche* over the parapet. I ask her if it's true that she'd been voted some sort of women of the year in the States and she blushes and says:

'Oh well, no, that was nothing.' I don't press her. I guess it's hard to take modeling awards seriously. But it's true that Peggy deserves an award because she's perfect. She's got her creams and sleep and preventive medicine and moderate exercise program and pragmatic optimism and fiber diet and everything in moderation and pragmatic except clean, down pat. Which doesn't leave much time for mistakes and men.

Prolific graffiti in the Beaux Arts john – just facing me on the seat, the lifesize head of a man, Robert Crumb-style, mouth wide open and balloon caption saying:

'Self-serve.'

First time out I'm taken aback by the spectacle of two thousand white invitation cards silently fanning their holders beneath a high vaulted ceiling covered in priceless frescoes. A crowded tropical fish bowl. I swim shyly down the podium.

All those multi-colored sequined embroidered jackets, hundreds of hours of work each, the price of a big house, wrenched off with less ceremony than a boxer peeling off his T-shirt after training, soaked with sweat, then stampeded, by my feet or someone's running past, undressing, re-dressing, like a speeded up film ran backwards, forward, backwards, forward . . .

I was often applauded, especially in the pink tweed high-tea-with-the-Queen number. Painless, even gratifying, for my first haute couture show in over a year.

Inès had said to me, sauntering in just in time to put on her first dress (she enters and exits on the right side of the podium; plebeians on the left):

'You see? I told you you would do Chanel.' She had told me nothing. We hadn't spoken in months.

'Maybe it's because of you?' I queried.

'No darling, it's because of *you*!'

'Thanks, darling.' I'd wondered why Karl Lagerfeld had suddenly decided to exhume my remains after years of hasty greetings at parties. Soon to be Queen Coco had used the old influence, in yet another act of exemplary behavior, thus saving her over-the-hill friend's pride with a magnanimous re-assurance of her ever constant and eternal worth.

Clye, that flippy young model from Düsseldorf who so got on my nerves, was here, coming up in the world. Asked me how old I was. I was about to tell her, hadn't I already? I always tell the truth, my age is one of my few proud possessions, though I don't enjoy the instant shock of young model's faces after pronouncing the high number, but she suddenly changed her mind:

'No! I don't want to know!' Her day had been too fairy-tale perfect to taint.

As I was leaving, Karl whispered to me that I had been the best one. I mumbled, oh, it was nothing, and fled, feeling as if I'd just received my very own modeling award. God, that man intimidates me. His culture and intelligence in the fashion world are as rare as a beaux arts building in a vacant lot, but you never know if he's going to blow hot or cold.

'Cut the crap, Karly. I'll bet you say that to all the girls.' Would that have been so difficult? And he would have laughed and I would have laughed with the easy assurance of the best ones.

Anne Marie and I half sit on a half wall outside, drinking champagne and snickering happily, watching the last of the audience leave. Regaining our sanity, glad it's over and that it went well. Not daring to wonder, not just now, why we're so lucky to be still doing it. When will the tumbling snowball run out of snow? Can't be bigger than a muffin now.

> Sublimated: 'You had to be Greta Garbo, mysterious, and not only that, sensual and ironic at the same time. In my head I had conversations with a truck driver. And I pretended to be Humphrey Bogart, which made me look like Greta . . .'
> 'Identification of a Top Model' – *Libération*

July 29, six p.m. Clic-Clac Studios: Press photos for a haute couture house. The near-sighted make-up artist has bad breath. Young, zealous, effeminate fat man. He squints at me:

'Look up pleathe . . .' I squint back and get warm stomach

problems wafted into my eyes and up my nose. I'd walked in late and everyone'd stared at me sullenly:

'Let's do it . . .' and pounced before my sweat dried. Foundation poured into my open pores.

He even smells bad chewing the gum I gave him, loudly in my face. Someone should tell him. I won't. Too much energy being diplomatic and he might be grateful.

'Your eyebrows are tho undithiplined!' he says. Tired old servants of luxury, plucked, colored, bleached and shaved. The few hairs left are as long as those of a silent movie villain.

'My eyebrows hate modeling.' I glance at him and know I should cut out my tongue. My stomach turns in fear of my anger.

Getting dressed I feel old, sweating under my falling buttocks.

'Try not to put your head up all the time,' the photographer says. 'We have some lovely pictures we won't be able to use because you're always putting your head up. You didn't do that last time.'

'Am I? That's funny. I usually feel better with it down.' Trying to fly through the roof as I can't seem to walk out the door. Forever. And not get paid? Think of a gulag, S. Look into the lens, it's not a machine gun. Beautiful, serene, sexy, touch of irony with the head down. It's better for the light, blinding me, scalding me, *look* at me mother fucker, come and get me you blurry shadow, *c'mon*, buy me a drink traveling salesman, sailor on the stinky zinc bar-top, five-days-sweat-dried hairy truckdriver I've been inviting for fifteen goddam years, come out of your goddamn dark corner and play eentsy-beentsy-spider up my waterspout legs, my legs spouting water, *Christ* it's hot, take me away! On your white-horse-Mack-truck-Porsche-rowboat . . .

I'd rather wash floors. I'd sweat less. This fur coat is too warm for Siberia. My pussy feels like it's in a boiling, overflowing *bain-marie*. Seriously, you won't see the sweat rivulets running down my legs? They won't make my legs

39

blurry? The fur toque is too small, there's no blood in my brain. No one wears a fur toque washing floors. Or peccary gloves. Or high heels for short people with club feet. Smashed in the middle. Daily model misery no one believes. They're too busy being jealous. Good. That's my pride. Let them wash floors. The hip my weight is on wants to snap out of its socket but if I shift the fur hairs will bristle and someone's going to come at me with the animal brush again and I'm going to whinny like a horse. Grit my thoroughbred teeth. Feet, head and hands, throbbing, swollen, serene, sexy, touch of irony and the head down. Fur hairs in my nose. Don't move, S. That's a sugar. You're a winner.

Two a.m: Purring CX Citroën, going home fast, hot summer night, a night to walk in the streets, slowly, lightbulb moon, looking for love, loving already. Dilated and vibrating. Happiness from out of nowhere. Out of the studio. Just living is a gift. I crane to see to the end of each shadowy street speeding past, I don't want to miss one single decor, noisy wind in my eyes and ears, washing me. I pretend I'm in Naples wearing a tight red skirt and high heels that fit, clack and echo on a dark empty street. I'm impatient to make love but too happy to care that I won't. Even impatience feels good tonight. I've just made a month's rent. I'm a privileged person.

November 14, 1983: Job for glasses. The client, fifty-year-old, steel-haired straight Robert, is being paternalistic, pretending to take my opinion seriously, asking me which pair of frames I prefer, they're all awful, thank you, as if he would choose the frames of my fancy to photograph, to hell with the marketing study. Then he starts trying them on me, and realizes that one of my eyebrows is higher than the other. One is above, one is below, his precious frames.

'This is very annoying,' he says, staring at my low eyebrow as if it were a sickness.

'Can't we do something?' he asks Etienne, the make-up artist. Soft-spoken, healthy, Rambo-esque, half Vietnamese and half French, Etienne fills in one of my eyebrows above itself, the other below itself. Make-up is a miracle.

We work outside in the courtyard. I am surrounded by the usual aluminum sun-gatherer on one side, have a tiny spotlight (twinkle) in one of my eyes from the front, and two people-sized, white styrofoam carton reflectors (circles-under-the-eyes chasers) on the other side – playing card soldiers out of *Alice in Wonderland*: OFF with her head for having those eyebrows! And there was bright light, can't be too beautiful. Boxed in and freezing, sitting on a stool; in the summer clothes they've put on me which I assume go with my summer glasses.

The concierge skulks past, chin first, flat-footed, with a broom, shooting poisonous glances at our suspicious group.

Etienne brushes my eyebrows every thirty seconds, a little over-conscientious. But he's cute, and he smells good. I scrutinize his eyebrows:

'You do it. Your eyebrows are perfectly symmetrical.'

The stylist is a middle-aged blonde who speaks to please, any one of twenty-five sentences she's memorized in her short life, like an anxious parrot. She'd lost her train of thought earlier voicing three thoughts in a row to explain why she liked my nail polish. I empathize. Her job too encourages drunk socializing more than learning new words. She starts accessorizing me on my stool, trying out this and that. My hands are getting purple with cold. Robert advises. Robert is wearing a loden. I am wearing a nylon blouse.

'It's a little thick, isn't it?' he says, meaning the pearls being placed around my neck. He wants his frames to be the only jewel. The stylist half hides the necklace under my blouse collar, and Robert keeps quiet for two whole minutes:

'It's, it's ... drooling ...' The pearls were falling more on to one side of my neck. I seem to be cock-eyed from top to bottom. The stylist changes the necklace.

Robert flutters in a semi-circle. I feel his desire to crush me into a wad of playdough and start over again, recreate me to go with his glasses. But he doesn't want to appear a fusspot, so he keeps disappearing. I don't know where and I don't look for him, knowing I'll soon feel the wind of his flapping hands even if he doesn't quite touch me, and see his smiling face, hiding his fear, too close to mine.

Robert has an enterprising junior partner in a navy-blue loden. Robert's is forest green. They are both standing one foot from my stool and staring at my eyebrow before the picture begins. Enterprising says:

'Try to imagine her in a natural position.'

An emotional huff escapes me. Try looking natural buddy, with six pairs of eyes like loaded gun barrels pointing at you. Because besides the two partners breathing on me, there is Etienne, the photographer, the stylist, and Volmar, the thin-shouldered hairdresser, with long wavy hair to his shoulders and Mona Lisa expressions, scattered throughout the court-yard, waiting for my eyebrow to change place. Fuck *you*, Navy-blue, even in a 'natural' position and *warm*, this is *it*.

We start the picture and, as I like obstacles up to a certain point, I start smiling.

'Don't smile,' says the photographer, a champion bowls player. Two rolls later, Robert appears with a new pair of frames and tries them on me:

'It's the same problem. It's so annoying . . .'

'Ah yes . . .' I sigh, commiserating. He takes the frames off my face, yanks an earpiece downwards brutally instead of breaking my neck, I suspect, and puts them back on me, too high up on my nose. One of the earpieces goes into an ear. He always puts an earpiece into an ear before getting it right. We start again and I open my eyes wide, trying to even out my face, which causes the frames to slip down a quarter inch.

'There's that eyebrow . . .' the traitor bowls player says and Robert jumps at the occasion to revoice his dissatisfaction:

'But it's the same problem! It's impossible!' I fix the frames myself, hurriedly. Please don't touch me Robert.

Navy-blue Enterprising decides to clear the air between rolls:

'She has an air of Christiane.'

'Does she?' says Robert.

'Who's Christiane?' I ask.

'Robert's daughter-in-law,' says Enterprising.

'You should have asked Christiane to do this. You would have saved money and I'll bet she's got great eyebrows.' I am past being diplomatic. We continue.

'Move your shoulders,' Bowls says, 'balance them differently. Put your hands in your pockets to make pleats in the coat.' I am wearing the stylist's raincoat now, and her pockets are full of dirty kleenex.

'Smile with your eyes,' he continues, which almost finishes me off. Now that I'm spitting angry, uptight, rigid with cold, and fearful of moving a single muscle because the pleats are perfect, knowing that asking for a cigarette or a pee will cause at least two heart attacks, he asks me to smile with my eyes no less, the easy way. How long have I been sitting motionless in the cold? An hour and a half? Think of the money, S. You are a professional, capable of smiling seductively, with your eyes, fulfilled or about to be, there's no doubt in the minds of the audience, while surrounded by nervous assholes. Click off, S., I'm here but I'm not. I can do anything because it's not me . . . poor imbecile.

Volmar has just returned from the neighborhood discount-store with lunch. I immediately ask for a glass of wine, take two great gulps with shivering hands. The glass almost slips from my frozen fingers.

Enterprising describes the mood of the last picture we will do:

'We'll need an *appealing* dynamic for the silhouette.' I ask for more wine and change clothes.

The 'silhouette' is done in the studio (my entire body as opposed to head and shoulders), on white background paper, walking in profile in front of the camera, twisting shoulders to face the objective in the critical middle: one, two, hallo! one, two.

Since I work less I drink less. The wine has gone to my head.

43

I go a little too far, my expressions almost grimaces, exaggerations of the wide-open-mouthed die-laughing photos in the various *Vogues* these days, as if the models were trying to convince anyone looking, the photographer or his cute assistant, that they had nice dick-sized mouths.

'Hey Robert! I've got this weight on my left cheek! They're symmetrical!'

'Good! Tell me if you stop feeling it.' Robert is so pleased with all my new movement, he dares to go to lunch, even offering me, gratis, a pair of glasses before he leaves:

'Don't forget your prescription. You have your prescription?'

'Yeah Rob, thanks, you're the greatest.' I wouldn't offer my grandmother his frames.

Bowls 'assures' the silhouette with two more rolls after Robert and partner leave.

'They didn't want to take you, you know,' he informs me when we've finished and are eating cheese and salami from the discount store.' But *I* knew you were the only one to do this!'

Another model arrives, to do, I don't doubt, the same picture, and I leave, drunk and disgusted, but not before I've finished my lunch.

Inkster, Michigan, December 30, 1983: You understand something important about America sitting and facing the breakfast bar in Big Boy's for an hour. 'ALL YOU CAN EAT: $2.75.'

I've been visiting my mother since Christmas and she keeps sending me away '. . . to relax . . .', '. . . take advantage of having a free babysitter for a few days . . .', but the real reason is that her husband can't stand me. So here I am observing my roots at 11 a.m. over a quart-size coffee in the nearly empty smoking section.

Solitary binger over there. Long thin straight brown hair in greasy strands, half-hiding hanging jowls and transparent-baby-blue-framed glasses, a polyester V-neck A-line turquoise dress strained at the seams and an expression, so defeated and mean, she's not even self-conscious, poised in front of her plate piled as high as the length of her face. She's flaunting it. America is full of these unattractive people with dirty hair, dressed as brightly as traffic lights, look at me! I don't care! Who should have done better and can't get beyond their bitterness, bingeing to soothing Muzak in roadside restaurants. We're right alongside Interstate 94.

There's another roly-poly filling up for the third time. She's sitting in back of me with an only slightly overweight man and they're discussing diets in between trips to the breakfast bar. She has thick black curls to her waist – no doubt her pride – unattractive glasses (maybe opticians unload their ugly frames on fat people), and her beach-ball body is clearly defined under skintight jeans. Flaunting it. More to love. Miss Curly, I'll admit though, has a certain grace, as fat people often do.

How many polka-dancing hamburgers and triple-chocolate-chip cookies are thrown at you in an hour of American television? How many hundreds of time a day? The entire country flaunts their land of plenty, 'all you can eat . . .' to whose shores they arrived starving and penniless. Not that there's no one starving, lazy bastards, let 'em croak, survival of the fittest, damn right. But nowadays people are also dying of excess, an apple a day keeps the doctor away so I'll eat ten and go on from there.

The two pizzas my mother ordered yesterday each came in paper packages as big as the kitchen table. I ate five pieces, half the table. It's easy! And finished up with half a bag of potato chips, paprika and onion, sitting next to my mother on the arm of her easy chair watching *Dynasty*. She finally gave in and took a few fistfuls. What could she do? I'd been crunching next to her for ten minutes, then the food advertising came on. Every ten minutes. Fifteen minutes of dancing food an hour.

Back to live bingeing in Big Boy's: a fat girl across the room has been staring morosely at me, or, I presume, at my skinniness. Finally says something to what looks like her young brother, who gets up and brings her back a plate of bacon, rolls and butter pats. And over there, with his back to me, hunched over his meal, pinhead, no neck, narrow shoulders and thorax widening out towards the stomach, maybe the butt's even bigger, a common American triangle. Fork-spearing coleslaw and french fries in side-plates at quick regular intervals, not really listening to the conversation at his table, eating is the business at hand, quickly, the fries will get cold. Can't talk either, he'd have to empty his mouth. He grunts, approval, disapproval.

My mother lost thirty pounds last year. She teaches a Weight Watcher's class twice a week. Successful weight watchers always teach the classes, as examples, visible proof that it's possible to lick bingeing in the land of giant pizzas.

I get up and buy a Bun Bar and a pack of Milk Duds from the vending machine for old time's sake. If I stayed here a month I'd gain ten pounds.

Bingeing is my sister's mortal enemy. I've never mentioned Janus, born in January when I was fourteen. The shit had already hit the fan so to speak, divorce proceedings were proceeding. She was my father's going-away-gift, though I honestly don't think he meant it. Crazy unnatural things happened after John F Kennedy was shot. A year after the Dallas crossroads the Moncurs hit theirs, in the sad-happy winter of 63–64.

My mother passed her final exams at the University of Michigan (halfway through her maelstrom marriage, she suspected she might need a decent job one day), gave birth to a second, healthy daughter as her husband was filing for divorce, and to clinch it, her father died, of delirium tremens coma. D.T.'s are a secret to keep forever in God-fearing suburbs and when I was fourteen I thought he was old so he died. I lived my entire life with such callous simplicity back then and I suspect a lot of people in the suburbs still do. I read about life's complexity in books, envying the sensitivity and reasoning powers of Holden Caulfield, Stephen Dedalus, Sebastian Knight. In fact as I was asking what Frank died of, this rare trip home, I realized that this was perhaps the first direct 'grown-up' question I'd asked about my own family. I also felt I was prying, and was hit with the old inertia, she won't answer me, and anyway I don't want to know.

Frank started drinking in the Marines when he found himself killing people. He'd emigrated to the States from a poor farm in Croatia to get a college education and got drafted instead. After his military service, he found himself a girl in Lorraine, Ohio, whose fidelity he soon doubted, so he went back to the farm in Croatia to get a 'good' girl.

Julia was pregnant on the boat back over. Frank went to work in the automobile factories. The stockmarket had just crashed, it was no time to start a family. With the advent of unions, Frank joined and was blacklisted as a communist for three years. Called a nigger lover because he made no bones about the fact that as far as he was concerned, a black man was just as capable of performing repetitious assembly-line motions as he was, that they probably had stomachs and had to eat, that he'd never noticed they smelled bad, and that he'd even had some interesting conversations with them.

He'd asked the local parish priest to vouch for him, at least say publicly he wasn't a communist (which was true), and the priest declined. Frank lost the faith and drank more. The college education'd been a drunk dream for a while. He was drunk every day at the end. I felt sorry for him and avoided him. He always told the same stories. He lived just long enough to see his daughter obtain her university degree. Needless to say, he was extremely proud of her.

My mother became a first-grade teacher. A few months after she started she took me to meet her class. I was unprepared for the violence of my reaction to my working mother. It was a sort of culmination of the last two years, the death throes, of her shitty marriage and our shitty home life.

Black kids and a few handicapped white children. I watched my mother helping a little boy with multiple sclerosis over the monkey bars and tears came to my eyes. Maybe the only kids she could find to teach were black and handicapped ones. I was white and pretty and she hadn't taught me anything, not even the facts of life, what does 'fuck' mean, mommy? Don't worry, I already know.

I watched her joking with the school principal, a hefty black woman, and noticed they had the same laugh, torsos tilting back and shaking rhythmically all over. My mother, a respected figure of authority, having a good laugh at the end of the day. I didn't recognize her. Their laughter was infectious. I laughed too, and cried, and hated her. She looked happier here than in the fourteen years she'd lived with me. But I was also proud of her and relieved. Hadn't her unhappiness been contagious and a source of guilt? I felt vertiginous with conflicting emotions. She'd made it. Out of the house and into the world, all on her own. *I* hadn't helped her. Now she worked with 'niggers'. I'd almost never been up close to one. Our community successfully protected itself against infiltration. But this black woman in front of me didn't look 'inferior'. She looked smart and happy and warm. She looked smarter and happier and warmer than most of the people I'd met in my white life.

The world became bigger. The other side of the tracks had just become an integral part. I imagined it as full of warm happy laughers. The hate and pity I was feeling didn't go away but became, momentarily, much less important in the face of the widening world. I defined my father, and my milieu, as racist.

I sulked on the way home, which my mother noticed and ignored. But I was also silently thanking her for one of the worst but most enlightening, exhilarating even, experiences she'd ever put me through.

I left home to be happy when Janus was four years old. I'd been a frequent and irritable babysitter. My mother was on her way to a master's degree in child psychology, specializing in abused children.

I'd been living in Paris for about a year when I received a letter from her apologizing for the way she'd brought me up. If she'd known then what she knew now . . . I wrote back an apology for not helping her in her time of need. Was it then that apologizing, just in case, became one of my golden rules and/or neurotic habits? In any case, my mother had just given me a sample of its impact. She'd embarrassed the hell out of me, which turned into an uneasy mixture of guilt, humility, and triumph – a lethal combination to inflict on anyone.

My sister Janus is an aerobics teacher and attends the nearby business university. We get along wonderfully well, even after years of almost indifference concerning each other's existence. We have, maybe not so surprisingly, a lot in common, even facial expressions. She is short and chubbyish, I am tall and skinnyish, but we still look alike. I spend a large part of my day in Big Boy's and Janus takes me bar-hopping at night. Our long catching-up conversations have been the best part of the trip so far. I care for Janus without having to deal with an entire range of love-hate contradictions, and feel protective of her well-being.

If truth, love, and praise-seeking are the reasons I come, and will always come home, this time it's manifested itself in an urgent need to show off my baby like I usually brag about my modeling career. I always return like a conquering heroine, apparently needing nothing. A baby was better than glossy photographs; palpable, warm and cuddly, their own flesh and blood. I wasn't sure my family understood about modeling, and why I did it in Europe. I didn't understand it myself. Had leaving home not been enough? I'd had to leave the country? No S., who *would*n't go to Paris if they got the chance? Europe appreciated my image and the States, which means New York as concerns modeling, didn't, that's all. But it was also true that my own country's indifference sometimes hurt, got erroneously mixed up with other muddy pains.

I'm spending a week in Michigan, then will visit my father and his wife (still Maureen the hairdresser) in Connecticut, where they'd moved to exactly the same kind of house they'd had in New Jersey. Then I have to be back in Paris to do a screen test for a movie called *Model Girl*. I couldn't have invented it.

My mother is being an admirable grandmother. I didn't quite know what to expect. Except for my infrequent trips home, we haven't kept in touch for the fourteen years I've been gone. We rarely write and never phoned before James was born. Other than the letter-apology event, she'd sent me *My Mother, My Self* a few years back, which I stubbornly refused to read. We hadn't come to each other's weddings.

She'd been doing fine on her own, teaching. Her mother looked after Janus during the day. Maybe she was lonely, she must have been, in this hypocrites' dead-end suburb, or thought Janus should have some masculine influence. (Her own dear father and mine met Janus when she was six years old. I introduced them on my first trip home.) Anyway, Vlada up and married Malcolm, an architect she'd met at a YMCA dance.

I'd married around the same time (Like Mother, Like Self), into an old French family whose members were as close as mine were far away. Pascal wanted me to stop dancing, stop modeling, and stop reading in bed at night. I stopped dancing, started fights about the reading, and continued modeling because he had to admit it was rash for a young couple to turn down all that money.

We took karate lesson together. Went to and gave dinners. Offered and received gifts. Decorated our home. I hadn't wanted to marry him. In fact I left after six months of living together and put a month's rent down on the second apartment I looked at. A furnished artist's studio with dark wood panelled walls, burgundy velvet drapes as long as theater curtains and art-deco furniture. A fairy-tale apartment. I imagined myself writing books like Colette, kneeling on the *prie-dieu* in front of the fire, and superstitiously averted my eyes from what had immediately become a sacred place, so as not to include it in the common transaction of apartment renting. Pascal visited me at the girlfriend's house I'd fled to and said something about suicide. It was easier to go back.

They didn't rub it in but I knew Pascal's parents had been shocked about my own not showing up for the wedding, nor offering to pay for it, nor even writing to introduce themselves to their daughter's in-laws to be. I'd thought nothing of it until I noticed their reaction, then was a little ashamed and felt a little sorry for myself, not much. What could I do? At least their son would no longer be living in sin. Wasn't that Pascal's main argument for marriage? Because our communal living bothered his family so much, especially the patriarchal grandmother in La Rochelle. It would make her so happy, and Pascal believed that making other people happy was just as important, if not more, than being happy oneself. I was trapped. No one was going to accuse me of weak moral fiber.

I was more passive as a wife than as a model. I did everything I was supposed to do, with a lot of well-intentioned help from the family. I imitated their motions, quickly joining in, letting them finish without me, keeping whatever they had accomplished clean. I was disgustingly meek. I was guilty, of having no idea how to act in the midst of the proud members of a very close family. To give them credit, Pascal's parents did what they could to help me relax. It was Pascal, who kept untiringly reminding me of the high class world of warmth he'd offered me, and organizing my work and my leisure like a missionary converting an ungrateful pagan who doesn't know what's good for her.

I fled, again, a hundred times more guilty, the house, the Labrador puppy, the cactuses, the Bentley, the forty-eight crystal-stemmed glasses: twelve bordeaux, twelve bourgogne, twelve champagne and twelve mineral water, the grandmother in her house by the sea, the parents' farm in Poitou, the parents, the son, the numerous social functions with their numerous traditions I called rules. I took my books and my records, after two years of marriage and a miscarriage, and moved into the apartment of a black dancer girlfriend who was leaving for New York. Dust to dust.

James is a success and it feels good to be here, except for Malcolm, whom I've noticed has started waiting for me to leave rooms before entering them. My mother is tender and tolerant, maybe she's always been. Julia is as melancholy and sentimental as usual. She cried when I presented James to her:

'Ooy! Ain't it! Ain't she beautiful!' because here was a great-grandchild from out of nowhere, but we would soon be leaving. She watched James getting into crushed banana and milk, and promises to give me lots of bananas to take back with us, in case there are none in France.

Janus visited me a few years ago, arrived with an extra suitcase full of toilet rolls, my mother's advice. Maybe I'd forgotten to buy paper when she and Malcolm had stayed in my apartment for a few days on their honeymoon.

I had just met M. when Janus arrived and was stupidly happy. 'Open Sesame', and you see the rock move. That's being in love. M. is a constant humming pain in me, but which dulls to calm at times since we've been here.

He drove us to the airport on Christmas day. Made me sit in the back with James, it's safer. He was tired. Had slept for three hours the night before. With whom? I didn't ask but ended up getting angry anyway. He won't fight so I fight for both of us, become a screaming banshee and he's the victim. I hate men who won't fight. My last words, hissed at him while rolling backwards inside the transparent plastic airport caterpillar: 'You're a hypocrite and a liar by omission!' are still poisoning me after a week. He won't move an inch, closer or further away. He won't say he doesn't love me, he won't hurt me, once and for all. I feel like a fish he'd found in an inner city stream, by accident, he wasn't even fishing that day he'd say, he was swimming, so why didn't he throw me back? I'm still on the polluted bank, half hidden in used condoms and candy wrappers. He comes back at night so no one will see him, not every night, I never know but I wait. He pours a cup of water down my throat while I gag and scream, bug-eyed and tail fin flapping.

January 7, 1984: Oh Dad dear Dad. I appreciate you repeating your invitation, saying to come and live with you if the going gets rough, but are sure you want your grandson? Crawling all over your dogs? You know it'd just turn everyone's life topsy-turvy – yours, mine, Maureen's, your Labrador Jay's, the German Shepherd Trixie's too. James'd love it, all that soft carpeting to crawl in . . .

The PIA plane is as full as the Christmas day plane was empty. I somehow manage to end up in an aisle seat with the middle seat empty except for a large Samsonite carry-on bag. Which I finally ask my fellow passenger to move after James has been squirming against it for a while trying to lie down. The man moves it three inches closer to himself, a barrier against the awful baby. So James will spend the trip sleeping like a foetus, his head smashed against the bag and his legs folded in my lap. He probably feels very secure. God knows, I may not have put my bag on the floor either before I was a mother, but now that I am, I see the world as peopled with grown-up comfort-seeking babies, and the part-time comfort-seeking baby I still am wants to sock them all in the eye.

Paris, January 8, 1984: I thought this was supposed to happen tomorrow. The screen test. I feel awful. Didn't sleep on the plane and there's just time to drop off the bags and James and leave again. I leave James with Premila, a young Mauritian girl I've employed since September, (illegally in France – so had I been for years), who is already James's second mother and sometimes mine, on whose trustworthiness and graceful sweet nature I am entirely dependent.

There is a text to memorize. I pace in a hallway for a half hour, experimenting in a whisper various ways of admitting to a murder, which is no way to rehearse. Then I go in, or rather, off. Right in front of Gérard Lanvin, gorgeous and famous

French actor. I tremble and cry, which is normal when admitting a crime, but I think I'm a little out of control. He grabs my shoulders as I finish in case I fall down. I look up at him, the accusing police inspector, and burst out laughing. His mouth is open and his eyes anxious. He thinks I'm really falling apart. So I'm convincing?

'You'll be okay! Really! I was like that too when I started, you should have seen me!' Like what, a perfect asshole? Even Gérard Lanvin? I could kiss him, he looks sincerely concerned, even if I think he's also trying not to laugh because I'd really looked like a perfect asshole; but I don't hold it against him.

'Next . . .' the cameraman says it delicately, I might still shatter leaving the set. I walk rigidly but make it. Where does all that emotion come from? No sleep and two weeks at home.

Afterwards we do group scenes. That's easier. Me and Inès de la Fressange, Anne Rohart, Violetta. But I'm not going to write my parents to brag about my screen test.

March 15, 1984: M. called, from a café on the rue de Rivoli. He said he'd waited for me outside the tent before the Gaultier show. I told him there was no reason for me to be there. Gaultier used kids. But I waited, he said. He asked about James. Fine thank you, he has chicken pox. But the fever's down. If you come to see him in the next few days, you'll see him full of red bumps. Even like that he's cute. I look for you in all the magazines, he said. What? I said. I look for you in all the magazines. I laughed. I thought you knew I was hardly in them any more. He said nothing and I laughed again. But I'm right here! Whenever you want! Hey, that's really crazy that you said that. We both laughed. He wants my blessing. He wants me to stop hurting so he can feel better. But that's always been the problem, Bronson. (M. looks like Charles Bronson but hates me to I say it.) They all look for the girl in the magazines, while I'm taking off my coat, while I'm cooking dinner, while I'm complaining and needing too much. They'll never find her. Princess Charming doesn't exist.

March 16: What makes me absolutely crazy, raving mad and frothing at the mouth, so impatient I can't listen to one single nonsensical stream of syllables out of the mouth of my son and try to decipher a meaning, is reading old diaries – how I *hope*, how I *hope* every time... the Ethiopian dancer, the Neapolitan surgeon, the French furniture designer, M., how the pages are full of hope and *waiting*. I spend months each time defending 'our love' to myself, that's suspicious already. Why doesn't 'our love' ever feel like enough? The doubt is always there but it's a joke in the beginning. The joke stays, the doubt becomes reality, 'our love' becomes the joke. S., you stupid butt asshole, anyone in their right mind, even taking into consideration that no one is in their right mind in love, any nincompoop doubts seriously before you do. Why don't you ever protect yourself? Against more or less insurmountable circumstances which are mostly that you're never as loved in return? Even before taking into account the fact that they often have other women. Why do you always have to go the whole hog? Do you think you're God? Will *you* ever permit yourself to be loved whole hog without finding it disgusting? You'd think you enjoy loving alone.

'How do you live this curious profession?'
S.M.: 'Like a melodramatic fairy-tale.'

L'Evènement de jeudi

Mexican dinner last night at Anne Marie's. Tracy did the cooking. Tracy, who is, was, my contemporary, and who's now living in California with her three-year-old daughter in a small house in her mother's backyard. She does make-up for television commercials. She's a woman now, no longer a model. You can tell, though I couldn't say how. Maybe because she seems unaware of her own physical presence, something models usually have a hard time forgetting if for no other reason than people stare at us a lot. We don't always do what we can to get stared at, but we do – maybe that's it – project. It's a way of existing. Tracy's stopped projecting.

She never looked very happy and she doesn't look happier. Although she says she feels much better than when she was modeling. Quitting the business was a necessity for her she says. It was that or a nervous breakdown. She's in Paris to start divorce proceedings with her French husband and father of her child. Getting rid of the last of the old life. The child doesn't seem any worse for wear. It's not the first time I've noticed an 'old' model's child normal and happy. With our fresh, first-hand experience of rejection, we seem to be extra careful with our kids.

Anne Marie's husband Stephen showed us movies, one of Wallis and me doing a Claude Montana show. I remember feeling ugly that day, old. I found myself young and pretty in the film. It was shortly after I'd left Pascal, five years ago, the fifth man before last.

Tracy says she misses the money the most. She lives on seven hundred dollars a month.

Had a horrendous, shouting insults ride home with a taxi-driver, because I mentioned he could have taken a shorter route. It happens to me often because of my accent, and after living here for fifteen years I find it tremendously irritating. He stopped his cab in front of Napoleon's tomb and ordered me to get out. I refused because I had James with me and Napoleon's tomb is nowhere near a cab stand. He screeched to a halt in front of my apartment building, screaming:

'Wouldn't even fuck you up the *ass*! Too *filthy*!' and the inevitable: '*Fuck* off where you *came* from!; He shoved James's basket-bed in an effort to get me out of his cab faster. I grabbed the basket away from him so violently James almost spilled out on to the pavement. He raced away almost before I could get a firm grip on the basket handles and step back. I sat down on the curb to calm down, let the barely-averted catastrophe sink in and go away. I am a guest in a foreign country, even if I've been living here for fifteen years. Some people don't like foreigners, they hate them and always will. They need their hate to exist. I mustn't need mine. Not like that. I am the mother of a small son and I must never allow myself such anger again. I could have killed James. With the help of a xenophobe imbecile but *I* would have suffered. Forever. Could I have even gone on living?

March 17: Project *Model Girl* bites the dust. I'm lucky. I can think they'd have taken me if it'd been made.

March 20: Life slow, cocoon-like, soft – don't want to hurt anymore or lose everything else.

I find myself regretting the intimacy I've had with lovers, as if too many of them knew too much about me and I want it all back (I wonder what I'd get if they gave it to me), for them to forget they ever knew someone like me.

Living in my dreams lately, it has happened, after dreaming, to be embarrassed by the reality of a situation, and what had been in my mind, an hour, a week before. Going back to adolescence, no, I forgot, I never left, going back to fantasy then, except when have I ever been real? When I hurt. The less I work, the less I exist. I'm exaggerating it on purpose. I don't even call people back. (You still answer the phone as full of hope.) It's not always disagreeable.

March 21: Fat woman at the market, harelip, dissolved before my eyes in what looked like an epileptic fit. She let out a terrifying loud moan. Light flashed and blinded me for a split second as it can when pain and fear take over by surprise. She hit her head on the ground falling, unconscious, was bleeding, trembling, body jolting spasmodically. I thought, her tongue, she mustn't swallow her tongue. I approached but didn't touch.

I watched her back. If it stopped moving that meant she'd stopped breathing, then I would look into her mouth. People were running. I asked a young girl in an apron:

'Do you have a telephone?'

'It's done,' she answered. Of course. People touching now. I kept watching her back, afraid to take my eyes off her. A passer-by told me she was in a trance. I responded with authority:

'No, it's epilepsy. It's *not* a trance.' She was breathing calmly now but still unconscious. I looked at the shopkeepers and shoppers standing around, all of whom were now avoiding each other's eyes, awkwardly waiting for this untimely reminder of pain and death to be removed from our midst. She was lying smack in the middle of the road, a showcase. I walked home slowly, feeling useless and concerned.

Recurrent dream, running in and out with the tide. I must follow exactly, it's exhausting, impossible. As close as I can get to the line of water without ever getting wet.

Recurrent dream of rectangles! Being dressed in them. No difference, no problem, tall rectangles. (Coffin clothes.)

March 25: rue du Faubourg St Honoré – where I live like an aging *jeune première* across the street from Grauman's Chinese theater.

Looking down, walking along, consciously avoiding faces, I start enjoying all the expensive shoes and accompanying perfumes. French and American. Estée Lauder's Youth Dew. Detroit smelled like that. Karen Graham advertised it for years, on hundreds of thousands of head-size double-page magazine spreads. I'll bet no one knows her name, although she was another feminine icon for the American collective unconscious.

Karen started her career in Manhattan's Bergdorf Goodman, where she was accosted by Eileen Ford, the inventor of modeling agencies. I was picked up by the same important person at the Third Avenue and Seventy-Ninth street bus-stop during the same autumn of '69. The man I was standing with, who wanted to marry me, told me not to call her; said she was just some lesbian who wanted my telephone number. But she didn't ask for my number I said. She asked me to call Ford's, her agency. He was the necessary comedown to what was otherwise the equivalent of being kissed by a prince and offered a kingdom. I knew who Eileen Ford was. I read *Seventeen* magazine. I was nineteen years old and dreamed of kingdoms. The man who wanted to marry me had just turned into a wicked witch.

I called my mother as soon as I got back to the apartment I was sharing with another Michigan emigrant who'd picked me up on a plane to Detroit to help pay the rent, not the smartest thing she'd ever done. I hesitated a week before calling Ford's, and when I went in, was not very kindly told to lose ten pounds and steam my blackheads every night for fifteen minutes, leaning over a casserole of boiling water with a towel draped over my head. Dreams coming true can lose their dream-like quality.

Karen and I did a test together a few months later (photographs taken to put together a portfolio, the model's, the photographer's, no one is paid, everyone's a beginner, the blind leading the blind), which is when we compared notes and discovered we'd been approached by Eileen around the same time. Which turned us into nervous competitors. I'm overly nice to my competitors. Karen disappeared to unattainable heights. Maybe now we'd get along. I'm sure she's still shopping in a Bergdorf's somewhere. I'm still waiting at busstops, on metro benches, waiting to be rediscovered, Frenchstyle, and that story makes me want to jump out of my skin. I've told it a thousand times and it sounds like I made it up.

August 19: Where I live in Paris is deserted on Friday nights in August. A no-man's land, center-city luxury-business district. When all the salesgirls and secretaries go home, and the businessmen join their wives on vacation, no weekday mistresses to dinner and romantic walks in the safe area around the dark offices, all you see are dog-piss tracks sloping down to the gutter. Pissy emptiness. At least the streets aren't straight. At least that squareness is spared me. But where do the dogs live? There aren't any people. It seems like there's just James and me and a few concierges, scrubbing the dog piss and rinsing the pavement with pails of ammonia water, thrown down behind me as if aimed for my ankles.

August 20: I feel like an abandoned city rat on this vacation Saturday in pigeon-grey Paris. I'm as skinny as a drug addict. I've been limping for a week. I think I broke a toe in dancing class without realizing it. Apparently this can happen. I limped with James in the stroller to the Champs-Elysées to buy a clock, as my beloved threw ours out our third floor window and I have had no idea of the time for three days, which bothers me immeasurably – a city rat in a timeless void. I used to enjoy correctly guessing the time.

We took a short cut through a shopping arcade and passed a self-conscious couple looking neither left nor right because they knew all eyes were on their fashionable selves. I said too loudly, passing them:

'You *stink* fashion,' then laughed nervously at the volume of my voice and the ridiculousness of what I'd just said. I didn't dare look back.

September 5: Fashion show for the radio. Is this job dumb? The models modeled and the designers commented into microphones. Marcello Mastroianni was there to push his play. I finally dared glance at him during my last passage. You and me baby, in a bomb shelter.

Walked home like I'm still modeling, tossing my freshly cut hair around, and pass my favorite bum, better looking than Marcello Mastroianni – a Tolstoyan hero, strikingly handsome, tall and wide, and an expression on his face which is the definition of melancholic. Cuts the grass under my feet every time. His 'absence' is a brutal wounding presence, and intimidates me. He knows I watch him. We watch each other when the other isn't looking.

He has a new bag, a woman's new brown plastic purse on one shoulder, the clasp broken and hanging down in a thin metal strip. The two battered Air France bags I already know. And a new pair of shoes, black leather lace-ups in good condition, which is a relief. His blue Adidas were really shot. His big hands are swollen and red, his face swollen and grey. Today he's not intimidating, he's acting like a normal bum. Muttering angrily to himself, reacting to the noise of cars and pneumatic drills. I pity him but feel almost disappointed.

I saw him a few months ago, I was on my way to the market, pushing James in his stroller – he knows James – accompanied by an American friend, Jeffrey, who had just arrived from the States. The boyfriend of a girlfriend, a Columbia graduate who couldn't find a job worthy of his dead languages diploma so he'd come to Paris to experience life and write poems about it on my couch.

He was about a hundred yards away on a park bench, commanding three times more attention than anyone else I know, taking up three times more space, sitting erect and watching me, wide-eyed, his mouth slightly open. As if I had betrayed him. He didn't seem conscious of the fact that I could see him looking at me like that, unveiled, breaking the rules. I wanted to run up to him, reassure him, shout at him, it's a friend, it's not what you think, but I passed by in silence, averting my eyes as soon as we drew near, hating my barriers.

Today is the first time I've seen him since. I suffered a moment of guilty responsibility for his deterioration, then felt stupid for overestimating my importance. I wonder what my life would be like if I had the courage of my impulses? Just having them doesn't mean anything. Yes, it's worse than not having them because once they're there and won't come out I'm forced to define the barriers: prudishness, cowardice, wanting to protect my high and low opinions of myself, wanting to stay in my safe tunnel. Self-flagellation is exhausting, is a backassed, masochistic form of pride and a hypocrite's replacement for not having that courage. I want to talk to him. I want to hear his story. I'm sure we have the most important things in the world in common. It can't be any more difficult than if, for example, I'd asked Marcello Mastroianni for his autograph. I could be sitting here proud of myself, my horizons widened and a better story to write. Or with no desire to write. I want to have the courage of my impulses. I worry about it more than about finding a job. It's the same worry. I want it to be the same worry. I mostly don't want to waste my time worrying about the person I want to be.

'Your agony is a luxury.' Who said that? That taxi-driver-actor I got talking to in London about Chekhov and Tom Stoppard, who calls me once a month at one o'clock in the morning to moralize about my easy life and tempt me with the suggestion that he come to Paris. I tell him to come but he wants me to beg. My agony is a luxury. Me and Tolstoy, sitting on it, til death do us never meet. Except Tolstoy gave me a sign. It was I who didn't have the courage, to talk to a bum. To talk to a stranger. To risk offending him. What would I say? Today he pretended he didn't know I was there; maybe he didn't. And perhaps – how can I not have thought of this before – his angry muttering to himself is a much more important sign of life than his, to me, esthetically pleasing 'absence' – one of the most important 'qualities' of a successful model! And I am as moved by his as I probably moved people by mine. That sounds dirty. I should have shouted at him: 'Bravo!! Bravo!! Encore!!!' Even if our mutually incoherent and angry mutterings never get us further than to the corner and back, it's something. And we see each other, even if our eyes don't meet.

'Beauty does not arouse compassion.' Who said that? Even if it gets run over by a truck.
    'Seduce a Top Model' – article in French *Vogue* for men.

October 15: Twice-yearly lunch with Norwegian Kia Melgaard, in from her New York penthouse on Concorde, *en exclusivité* for Azzedine Alaïa and whoever hears she's here. Kia makes about twenty-five times more money than I do, and looks like a slant-eyed, better-muscled version of the long-haired adolescent in *Death in Venice*. She's one of my very best friends. I treasure her like a jewel I'm afraid to wear too often for fear of losing it, and I don't, I hardly ever see her. I don't quite trust her friendship. I'm sure she doesn't quite trust mine. Models are very insecure. We'll see when we're no longer modeling. We're drinking buddies and each other's best audience. There's a competitive side to our relationship: who is going to be the funniest most intelligent one today? We're not sympathetic to each other's suffering unless it happens to coincide. I think we might each suspect the other of never having really suffered, even of being a spoiled brat, 'wasting' her 'talent' on men and miming ideal women. And yet, we spend the entire first part of our time together proving to each other that we have suffered: dissecting, making fun of, deploring the business and our love affairs, working gradually towards the point where we're sure we've been believed. Because if I can't understand and trust Kia, if she can't understand and trust me, perfectly, given our similar careers, then no one can. And in that case, *why* do we keep trying to make everybody, but *everybody*, understand us? Why do we seek absolution? Because people never absolve us of the sin of being conscious of our beauty and 'using' it against the unbeautiful, getting rich on what they'll never have but must look at in magazine pages. They mock our so-called arguments, our claim to existential and physical suffering followed by obsolescence and old age at thirty, and are convinced we spend all our time in front of mirrors, cameras, and fucking photographers, in narcissistic symbiosis. They can't deny the early end of our careers but consider it just punishment. What is interesting is that we do the same thing to each other, the ritual cross-examination, confession and absolution, of one model by and for another, which nullifies, or at least alleviates, the non-absolution of the world of decent citizens. We test each other through *their* eyes, until our mutual instability and peculiar *mal-de-vivre* recognize each other, until our conversation becomes a series of echoes, and we are, once again, incalculably grateful for each other's existence. Then we make sure that the other is not making too many mistakes in her evolution, or at least that we are making the same ones (not our fault), and that we still agree on the important issues, love and revolt, even if neither of us has revolted yet except in our mutual conversations, and our love lives are the proof of confusion. And we laugh, hysterically, that more than anything, in what is perhaps one of the most perfect harmonies either of us will ever find.

Today she gave me advice:

'Your problem now is finding, and *accepting*, a job where you'll have responsibility. I mean, all we've had to do until now is just *arrive* and *complain*.'

December 24: I'm giving a Christmas dinner for James's nanny Premila, her husband Prem, her brother Sam and Sam's wife Sheila, her sister Moon and Moon's boyfriend Pravin, her cousin Jacques and his wife Mala and their little boy Kavi; Errol Sawyer, a black American photographer; Victoria, a Russian make-up artist and her son Vadim; and an Australian tourist who's coming with Errol. We're having fish curry. Premila's making it. Premila, in fact, is giving the dinner, in my house.

After dinner we all danced to The 64 Greatest Motown Original Hits. James was half-dragged, half-carried around the floor by the six-year-old daughter of someone I've forgotten to mention. Romeo! How can I have forgotten a name like that? And Rumina, his daughter, both vaguely related to Premila, or not, it's just the same. Immigrant Mauritians stick together in Paris, they have to. They've even organized their own 'bank', which lends money to members on a no interest, trust only basis. If someone buys a house, everyone else helps with the down payment. If someone dies, everyone chips in for the funeral. I admire them and am envious and, as an assimilated and legal resident of French society, am completely alone in comparison. But tonight I took pictures and felt family. It was a great success.

> 'At eighteen, you leave your Detroit suburb. Wasn't your arrival in New York a cold shower?'
> S.M.: 'Completely. And I was so stupid, so unbelievably naive. I didn't know how to say no, so I got non-stop fucked, literally fucked . . .'
> interview in L'Evènement de jeudi

Manhattan, July '68: Things happen to naive people. A man I'd just met took me to lunch, spoke kindly to me like a father, and informed me that if I wanted to make it to the top like Jean Shrimpton and Twiggy, I'd have to do it with farm animals. Plus all the make-up lessons, eating and drinking and dressing lessons he'd have to give me. He made me feel guilty for not knowing these things already. I didn't even know that I didn't know. And how lucky I was to have met him. But I'd have to be very conscientious, deserve the attention, if he decided to take me on.

I was working in the garment district as a receptionist, a small dingy office, fifty-five dollars a week after taxes. It had been the first job I'd applied for and I was surprised to get it because I couldn't even type. I'd just spent a year at Wayne State, failing most of my classes and losing my scholarships. I'd participated in an experimental college for students who knew how to study on their own. Class attendance was not required. So I never went to class. My father still lived in New Jersey. I thought I could live with him for the summer, commute into New York and make enough money for my second year, which would be my first year over again. I lost my first paycheck the night I got it, somewhere between the small dingy office and the Port Authority Bus Terminal.

I'd had the job about a week when I got a phone call from a 'model talent scout' who'd seen me around. I wore a lot of make-up and turquoise contact lens, and sought people's eyes walking down the street. He invited me to lunch, ending the conversation with what sounded like a scolding:

'Don't be late!'

I knew I probably shouldn't go, some authoritative stranger asking me to lunch over the phone. But I had just turned nineteen, had not seen a lot of life and was dying to. 'Life' was the big city and the big city was New York. All the rest was imitation. People were starting to tell me I should be a model. I dreamed about modeling the way little girls play with their Barbie dolls, pretending to be her. I was a big girl now. I could handle it. And maybe that's how things worked here. I didn't know how things worked.

The address I'd been given turned out to be an elegant French restaurant. I had never been in one before, French or otherwise, unless you consider The Western House in East Detroit, with twelve-foot steer horns over the self-serve counter, an elegant restaurant. I'd never drunk white wine or eaten fresh fish that looked like a fish.

Rule number one, said Maurice, which was the talent scout's name: drink only white wine, it's better for your health, and eat lots of fresh fish. He was fat and fifty, accompanied by a luscious silent blonde, and a tanned hook-nosed Mafioso type of around forty, who never opened his mouth.

Maurice filled my glass a few times before throwing the animals at me. How did I think they got to where they were? They weren't prettier than I was. I got a sinking feeling. Was life like this? And started feeling sorry for Jean Shrimpton and Twiggy and everyone very successful. Maybe all successful people did it with farm animals. Maybe for them it was normal. Maybe it was an acquired taste like the raw oysters everyone at the table was swallowing and I'd declined to sample, more out of fear of not looking dignified with my mouth open than fear of the live animal. How did one keep one's dignity while fucking a goat? Being very successful must take care of everything.

Maurice suggested I phone my office, pretend a doctor's appointment, say I wouldn't be in for the rest of the afternoon. I was going to get my first modeling lesson.

On our way to wherever we were going – the other two had disappeared without saying goodbye but then they had never said hello – Maurice asked me in a very confidential, solicitous tone of voice if I thought I was capable of masturbating in front of him. That a model's job was to please people, the right people, and he knew what the right people liked. He knew them personally. I said I thought I could do that.

I was a little afraid in the elevator of the building we entered. Was it going to happen now? I imagined straw in the bathroom. And fur in my mouth. And sometimes it bloated I'd heard, you couldn't get it out. I felt challenged. This man was disgusting but his fatherly tone of voice got to me. I was more unsure of myself, of not being up to the task, than frightened.

We entered a big beige apartment, almost empty, with thick stained carpeting. Maurice got on the phone in the living room and I practiced in the bedroom, masturbation is such an ugly word, then did it in front of him, me who wouldn't eat an oyster. He was sitting in the only chair. He slowly took off his shirt with one hand, while the fatty spread fingers of his other hand laid over the telephone speaker into which he murmured. I really tried, I forced myself, I did it badly and couldn't believe I was doing it. I was on the verge of racing out every second, but I stayed and kept doing it.

Then the men he'd been phoning started arriving. One-thirty in the afternoon until nine-thirty at night. I didn't see the second one approaching because the first one was on me. I think there were five in all. After the shock of the first body, hairy like an animal's, I started to feel angry but fought it down because now I was afraid. I concentrated on the movements, made whatever they wanted to do to me easy for them. I made little noises to fake pleasure. I watched myself from above, one sex between my legs, another in my mouth; the sensation of separation was exhilarating. I was grateful there were no animals. In the beginning I'd half waited to hear one come trotting over to the bed, except I suppose if he really wanted me to do it with dogs and goats, he'd have said I had to do it with horses and cows.

I remember nothing after the first few hours. Except I was exhausted, I almost couldn't go on. But I didn't want to stop.

Many years later I ran a long distance on a karate weekend, with a husband who believed in sharing everything. I'd never run a long distance. The master made fun of my panting, of the bandana I'd tied around the back of my head. It was the middle of winter and he thought I was trying to keep warm. We were there to be pushed beyond our miserably low limits, not to be comfortable. I spit at him between my teeth:

'It's to keep my glasses on . . .'

'Oh . . .' he said, surprised at my violence and the pragmatism of my words. I ran all seven kilometers, like the men, some of whom had had ten years of training.

In these circumstances too I would be above reproach. I would go to the end of it. I didn't want to, or did I? It was something, better than reading about it in books and made to think it was exciting. Aren't the 'dirty' ones the ones who never do anything because they don't dare? Or are they the ones who can't do anything unless it's dirty? And I needed to be graceful. No one was going to criticize my lovemaking, body lending, whatever I was doing, being a hole. Then I could tell him, them, anyone, I made a mistake and you're a scummy bastard. Because then I'd know what I was talking about.

About nine in the evening a woman arrived, who took off her clothes and started rolling joints. She didn't say anything, pay attention to anyone, just stood up in the bedroom naked and rolled joints on a dresser top. I took one puff, maybe two, and 'came to my senses'. I jumped off the bed and started yelling at Maurice, who never did anything after taking his shirt off: not a pretty sight. I screamed at him to put his shirt back on, he was ugly, he was going to miss the last bus to Brooklyn or Trenton, his wife was waiting for him, the poor bitch. I felt powerful when I started yelling. I vaguely remember Maurice getting nervous. Then I fainted. You didn't feed me enough model food, fatso. Fish and white wine are no good. Maybe I should be a steak, mashed potatoes and salad 'model'. All those steaks up my cunt on my first assignment. You're a tough master, fatso. I wish I had said that.

I awoke the next morning in a wilderness of empty bed. I opened my eyes without moving, the room was flooded with sunlight. I turned my head toward the window and encountered the Mafioso-type leaning on an elbow and staring at me. A vision. Had he been one of them? He prudishly pulled the wrinkled white sheet we weren't sharing up under his shoulders and held it there; a Roman in a toga. We didn't speak.

I dragged myself to the bathroom, my muscles as sore as after ten karate lessons in a row. Years later I would say I'm so sore from karate class it feels like I got fucked by ten men in an afternoon. I leaned on the sink and gazed at myself in the mirror. I didn't recognize my expression. I was surprised to see myself so well. I'd slept in my contact lens. My cheeks were sunken. I must have lost five pounds. One false eyelash was still half glued on. I took a pee and discovered the crushed tampax that had been in me all that time. I tried to wash and dress quickly but my movements were slow.

The Mafioso-type handed me two ten dollar bills for a taxi. He had his pants on but no shirt. I stared at his neck and handed one of the bills back. He pushed my hand away with a gesture of irritation and I left. I was worried about showing up for work in the same dress as the previous day. My boss will know I hadn't gone home. He'll guess what I've done. He'll see, smell, the men on me. Or think I'm a slob for not changing clothes.

I can't remember if I called my father. I suppose I must have, telling him I'd spent the night with a girlfriend. He never asked for details. I was old enough to know what I was doing. I called someone later that morning, a man I'd just met but trusted, he'd said he loved me, and told I him what'd happened. I was trying to find out without asking what to think because I still didn't know. He laughed and laughed and said he couldn't believe it. He hadn't thought I was such a stupid bitch. I hung up on him.

Maurice called me the next day and asked if I were free for dinner, just me and him. I hung up on him.

I saw the Mafioso type five years later in a bar. He snickered at me from across the room. I wanted to go up and murder him, but I just left.

Paris, November 1969: Jacob, the tall black muscular photographer in thick prescription ray-bans, who had brought me to Europe to be photographed in John Meyer of Norwich ready-to-wear, his only big client and my first big job, and with whom I was no longer on speaking terms, had given me two suggestions before forgetting me forever. The first was to change my hotel:

'This place is expensive and the job's over. The client's through paying and I've had enough of you, girl. I'm here to play and you're too much *work*.'

We had spent a tense moment a week earlier on the edge of a cliff in Ibiza, hissing at each other with gin-and-tonic courage. One more word out of me and I was going to find myself wingless and flying:

'You see them, wasp-girl? You see those waves and rocks?' And I reciprocated with the oath that he was coming with me, daring him to lay his black and white mitts on me, my dead body would be at the expense of his mother-sucking own.

I had taken to imitating Jacob's vocabulary and gin drinking in defense and admiration. I was desperately unhappy about being seemingly unable to do anything to please him. Jacob was an equal rights militant who read a lot. He'd spent ten days in a Detroit jail during the summer riots in '67, his cameras and films confiscated. (From my suburb a half hour away, I'd watched the fires burning and listened to the mounting death toll on television as if it were happening in Bolivia.) He'd marched in Chicago in the summer of '66 with Martin Luther King, which is where he learned the song he sang twenty times a day:

'Oh I wish I were an Alabama trooper, That's what I would truly like to be; I wish I were an Alabama trooper, 'Cause then I could kill the niggers legally . . .' sometimes grabbing my chin and looking deep into my eyes as he sang, for signs of deep-rooted prejudice. He wanted to succeed in the racist American fashion industry as a Black Man. Forehead, thigh-slapping, gin and Pall Mall, he orated nightly wherever he was, mostly Max's Kansas City. Charismatic disgusted soliloquies on the mother-sucking injustice of the world.

Many people admired Jacob, including the client on this trip: a short, mean, insignificant, beak-nosed, whiny-voiced bleached blonde with a bubble-cut, with whom he was sharing his room.

After screaming at and insulting me during five or six testing sessions in his studio, Jacob said that if I didn't get better on the job he'd send me home. So why did he take me?

I was ecstatic. After seeing every new photographer in the city three times, and leaving numerous composites (a model's calling card, pictures instead of words) on a corner of the reception desks of the successful famous ones, ready to be thrown into the evening trash, I had eaten a lot of free meals and slept with about fifty men (not only photographers, I got picked up in the street a lot), but had only two published photographs in my portfolio. Before I met Jacob, I was about to slink back to Michigan and good old Wayne State. If I hadn't left yet it was because I kept avoiding thinking about how I would pay for my failure. Failing in America is about the worst thing that can happen to you.

I'd had an abortion, they were not legal yet, a week before we took the plane to Spain, in the hotel basement office of a pig-faced doctor in Pittsburgh who had just gotten out of prison for performing illegal abortions. The experienced girlfriend who'd found me the butcher warned me:

'If he doesn't give you an anesthetic, don't let him touch you.'

'Anesthetic!' cried the pig. 'You'll be here for three hours getting over it. I want you out of here in twenty minutes.' And I was, walking gingerly.

I didn't know who the father was. The man from whom I'd borrowed the money, the solvent one of three possibilities, knew I was lying when I said it was him – I'm a guilty-faced liar – but handed me six hundred dollars, smiling wryly. I knew I would probably never see him again and was a little overwhelmed with how little I cared, with the cold-heartedness with which I was making the arrangements and would carry them through.

A photographer friend had kindly offered to meet my plane from Pittsburgh. I'd half expected him not to show up; I didn't know him that well. He brought me to his apartment, fed me vegetable soup and put me to bed. I didn't think he liked girls, so if I wasn't surprised when he started caressing my head, I was when he started kissing me. Technically we didn't perform the act, which under the circumstances would have been extremely foolish and hurt like hell, but it was better than most of the acts I'd performed.

I was an ace at discounting every real thing that came my way so I never saw him again.

Jacob arranged for a Cadillac limousine to drive us to the airport. He had it stop in front of Max's Kansas City to flaunt our getaway and drink the last drink on American soil. He held up his battered passport, not battered from use but from being in his pocket all the time, baptized it in gin, then me, the male model, the client, and gazed at us lovingly while the crowd at the bar applauded. I was solemn.

We left New York at midnight, arrived at the Barcelona Ritz in the middle of the next afternoon. Everyone else went straight to sleep and I went for a walk, feeling as weak-kneed as if I'd just been released from prison after a twenty-year sentence for being born.

A hundred yards out the gilded door, someone was calling my name, then an arm was waving in a wide up-and-down arc, as if it were attached to a stick that an invisible puppeteer was manouvering from the back seat of an approaching taxi. A drowning arm. Then a horizontal head laid on top of the arm, smiling widely. Ricky. My French Mediterranean, easy-going, television producer 'boyfriend' had arrived from Tunisia. I hadn't seen him in two months. He'd sent me a telegram the week before that I was just now thinking I should have read more carefully. Easy-going and guaranteed to irritate Jacob's militant black seriousness.

Jacob is one of those photographers who like to possess his girls entirely, form them from scratch and high potential, then place them on hard won pedestals. I thought something must be wrong with me, other than the things he'd already mentioned, because he'd never tried sleeping with me. Everyone tried sleeping with me and usually did. I think he hated me too much, and he couldn't sleep with everyone. He never even touched me, only my shoulders once, trying to shake out an expression.

Ricky left the next day but the damage was done. Jacob was sure I'd arranged the meeting and I didn't contradict him because the truth sounded worse. Yes, I vaguely remember writing and telling him I'd be in Barcelona. He sent me a telegram I didn't bother understanding. I never thought he'd actually show up. Travel halfway around the world to spend the night with me. I didn't think he liked me so much.

My passivity was a problem. Many men 'fell in love' with my docile nature and bedroom gymnastics. I was so cowed by all their attentions, not only did I submit to them, I tried very hard to merit them. And although being a model and more specifically, wearing mini-skirts, dance leotards and Swedish clogs, is 'asking for it,' I dressed like that because I wanted to be photographed, not fucked. I wanted the power of seduction, not to be seduced. I wanted an identity, the identity of visual symbol – a perfectly satisfying identity for shy narcissists seeking the existential recognition they can't give themselves.

All my romantic adventures started out with my being pleased and overly grateful, if less and less surprised and soon afterwards, cold and irritable. The only satisfactions were eating well and knowing I'd given a decent blow job. Latin Ricky was no exception. Here I was, independent and about to make a large sum of money for the first time in my life, and a man shows up. Even if he was a television producer, I knew he'd never give me a job. Men who fall in love with docile natures don't take risks, don't give a new model her first break. He was just a man, equals just fucking, and I'd had my fill.

For the next two weeks, Jacob changed location often and re-shot each photograph in each new setting. What I was lacking in mystery, maturity, and seduction, would perhaps be compensated for in sunsets, waves, mountains and palm trees.

The male model, Ricardo, another Ricky, comforted me, listened patiently to my self-examination-accusation monologues in the hotel hallway after work. Which often ended in tears; he'd put an arm around my shoulder and pull me to him. He eventually invited me to his room.

I blotted all my frustrated desire to please against this beautiful man's understanding body like an erotically precocious two-year-old. He turned his face away from mine and covered his sex. I guess he'd just wanted to talk. Maybe he hadn't even invited me to his room. Maybe I'd misunderstood. The world was still a confusing place.

The next day, Ricardo-Ricky and Jacob were both kind to me. They must have talked I thought, hating them both and myself a little less for once. Jacob's afraid I'll go to pieces and he can't afford to send for another girl from New York. I was almost grateful to the client for not masking her contempt, for not *ever* being nice, and ignoring me the rest of the time. She'd hand me the skirt to be photographed between two fingers at the end of an outstretched arm, sometimes letting it drop before I could grab it. I drank gin all that day and Jacob complimented a few of my expressions.

At dinner that evening, Ricardo-Ricky talked about his traveling. He hadn't done much, the States and London. He'd really adored London and wanted to go back. He had friends there who could put him up. But it would have to be another time because he was broke and wasn't it frustrating, being so close to a place you loved and unable to get there? I asked him how much he needed and lent him two of my three hundred dollars.

Salvador Dali was staying at the Ritz. He looked unreal, standing in the exact middle of the round lobby, twirling his mustache and leaning on a silver-knobbed cane, performing Salvador Dali. I'd never encountered, what was for me, the improbable reality of a myth. It was like seeing Mickey Mouse. And he watched me, from the center of his mandala, staring ostentatiously as I asked for my key. Then followed me, with another man who looked and acted like Zorro's deaf-mute sidekick, Bernardo, down the somber long hallways of the hotel's upper floors, playing hide-and-seek. They actually hid behind columns when I looked behind me. Loony Toons. But that was it. Nothing happened. They followed me twice at a suspenseful distance. My surrealist introduction to the Old World.

Jacob's favorite model is to modeling what Greta Garbo is to the movies: Donna Mitchell. Enormous, droopy, dreamy eyes, an inch of visible eyelid when her eyes are open, plus white under the pupils. He kept holding her up to me as a role model. I spent two weeks trying to get white under my pupils, pushing them up into my eyeball sockets while keeping my eyelids half closed, ideally lengthening them, thus giving my face that everything you ever dreamed of in a woman, mostly mystery and sexual tricks, you want to drown in expression. Which must have made me look drunk even when I wasn't. Fifteen years later, I still think I was almost pushed off that cliff.

When we got to Paris, Jacob suggested eating at La Coupole. I would certainly see people I knew. As I had no other advice to follow, I followed Jacob's.

I realize now that Jacob talked to me as if I already knew a lot of things I didn't. Like exactly who Yves St Laurent was, that it was easy to find drugs on Formentera, maybe I should try modeling on drugs, that all the artists in Paris lived in Montparnasse, or how to deliver this year's model expressions as if I'd been born looking at people like that – all the knowledge I too would take for granted in a few years. My nodding incomprehension, along with Jacob's constantly recovering from hangovers, drove him completely nuts. He wanted a whiz kid and I'm a slow learner.

I was planning to stay in Paris for a few months, if there was work. Then, as now, American beginners were encouraged by their agents to spend some time in a large European city, usually Paris or Milan, to acquire *savoir-vivre*. And collect 'artistic' pictures, ideally a cover of *Elle* or Italian *Vogue* or both, before returning to New York's high-pressure competition and assembly-line four jobs a day. Fifteen minutes late in New York, a model pays for everyone she's kept waiting. And on time can make so much money she's obliged to become a corporation for tax purposes. It was worth training for. There were fewer models in Europe. They were paid less than half the New York prices. Everyone arrived late on jobs, and it was normal for certain photographers like Sarah Moon or Guy Bourdin to take all day to shoot one photograph, or not shoot at all because the light wasn't perfect. There was time to learn, to nuance expressions and positions, to talk, to drink, to dream. In many ways it was a dream-come-true life. Or would be in nine months. I still had some fumbling to do before I got lucky.

I moved to an inexpensive hotel on rue de la Tour, Paris 16. Everything in my new cheap room was dark-red and dirty, the carpeting, the thick velvet bedspread, the matching dusty drapes on the window and surrounding the bed. And it smelled like a locker room.

Every new hotel is a new chance, the possibility of a new life, at least a new experience. Having to begin it on top of the stains and smells of previous lives has always upset me, especially this most important first time on my own.

And why had I been given a dark-red room? Maybe the concierge of the other hotel who had made me the reservation had told them here that I was probably a prostitute because I'd had hot words in the lobby with a black man and a bleached blonde.

The walnut furniture was old and scratched. The toilet was in the hall, which couldn't be normal. It was like a bedroom without a bed. During the day was different, in offices, department stores, restaurants, you were a public person using public facilities. But at night! Waking from your private sleep and having to *dress* to go to a public toilet! The pale old man who had brought up my bag had indicated the 'water closet' in passing:

'Double V.C.' he kept repeating and pointing to a door, yes, is this my room? I had no idea what he was saying, it sounded Polish, until he showed me.

I hadn't moved since he'd left, except for locking the door after him and realizing you could see into the hall, and so into the room, from the keyhole. I stood still, out of the line of vision of the keyhole, trying to comprehend what struck me as the fake luxury of a ghetto room, staring mostly at the canopy bed, where I could imagine smothering but not sleeping, a damp spongy pit of fungused feet, menstrual blood, sperm, urine, shit streaks and sweat, inside light-proof canopy drapes . . . my breathing and ringing ears were suddenly as loud as passing trains. I experienced a sort of waking vision of myself as total weakness, total incapacity to cope. I swayed, or the bed beckoned. I left my bag and fled.

I felt euphoric in the metro, one extreme to another, which I had miraculously taken in the right direction, since the train was going over the Seine. Beautiful postcard Paris at my feet, life-size, in three dimensions. It was the first time I'd been in a foreign country where I not only didn't speak the language – chaise, haricot vert, la salle de classe, jaune, bleu, rouge, two years of high school French, I even got bonjour and bonsoir confused – I didn't know anybody except two people who wouldn't talk to me. Ricardo-Ricky was in his beloved London. The ugly client had rarely deigned more than a grunt, and the last sentence Jacob had managed was an explanation of how to get to La Coupole, like I already knew Paris. I found it because I had to. Having a hundred dollars to my name didn't phase me. Europe was cheap, a hundred dollars was a fortune.

I ate dinner at six p.m. in a corner near the kitchen with my back to most of the room. I hadn't expected it to be as big as a railroad station. I didn't dare turn around and look for my friends but somehow doubted they were there. I was slowly invaded by the certainty that I would never find my way back. I didn't want to. I felt almost safe sitting down in a crowd but now that I'd finished eating I no longer had the right to be here. I couldn't remember if the metro was to the right or the left out the door. My face started getting hot and the restaurant noisier. I quickly turned and looked behind me to avoid crying and saw Jacob, sauntering between the tables looking unsure of himself. He saw me out of the corner of an eye and turned away. I turned back and called a waiter as I might have screamed for help. I showed him my metro map, hoping he'd feel sorry for me, pointing to where I'd come from and asking in baby English how to get back. He said something in quick irritated French and left. I nodded to his receding back, folded my hands in my lap and stared straight ahead of me.

There have been times when I have been infinitely grateful for being pretty; the bearded man eating oysters on my left, turned to me and inquired in perfect English if I needed help. I said I was fine. He asked if this were my first time in Paris. I started talking with mixed feelings: disagreeable déjà-vu, another man, I can't stand it, but which prevented me from sounding too desperate, and relief, I was saved.

The only thing I remember him saying before his being amazed that I'd never heard of Castel's, was that he'd just lost five kilos by simply cutting wine out of his diet. He was visibly pleased with himself but his statement upset me. Here was something else I didn't understand, about wine. I had recently discovered it and loved the courage it gave me, even if the wine courage was slower coming than gin and whiskey courage. Wine drinkers were more acceptable than hard liquor drinkers, and I was more worried about being acceptable than anything else. I could drink with a gin drinker, I couldn't *not* drink gin with a gin drinker, but on my own, wine would be safer for my reputation. Except if it made me gain weight. Models had to be skinny. So I'd have to choose, between being skinny and frightened, or fat and courageous? Five kilos was over ten pounds!

The first man I meet in Paris and his name is Pierre. He took me to Castel's, which turned out to be a dark red discotheque with a pillbox for a dance floor, on which habitués were self-consciously moving their upper arms like broken bird's wings and walking in place to old fashioned rock 'n' roll. I drank whiskey and coca-cola, following Pierre's advice, quickly, for the effect. I believed and acted upon most of the advice I received, and went out on to the pillbox, feeling deliciously euphoric and superior, even in my wheat-gold corduroy slacks and loafers, jabbing people with my elbows, trying to get a little room, wanting to show off in front of my saviour, give him his money's worth. We danced a few slows to 'Lay Lady Lay' which came on every three records, and Pierre drove me to his unfurnished, unfinished, unheated, attic apartment. A construction site. Which was fine. It smelled like freshly cut wood, not feet, not dust. No stains, no history.

I think it never crossed my mind that I must have made men feel virile. Pierre was no beauty, they often weren't. I concentrated on the man's pleasure because mine was too difficult. Don't people have a tendency to assume that the sexual pleasure they are receiving is shared? Even if their partner doesn't try hard to make them think it, which I did that night, since I was especially grateful. And the more active one is, the less one must passively endure.

The following day he took me visiting (look what I found and laid immediately!) to the small attic apartment of a young friend of his – everyone in Paris lived in attics – who took us to my idea of a French restaurant for lunch. Small separate tables covered in red and white checkered tablecloths, not all lined up one against the other like in last night's canteen. Pierre and Benoit, the friend, reminisced about the good old days, May '68, when one could spend part of the evening throwing rocks at policemen, then go drink whiskey at Castel's, which was only a few blocks from the Revolution's center. War and peace, revolt and relax, perfect equilibrium. It was my ignorance of the event that started them off, a mere two weeks out of isolationist America where I never, anyway, read the newspapers. They kept lapsing into French and I watched them, not understanding a word and perfectly happy.

After lunch Pierre took me driving around St Germain des Prés, looking for a new hotel. He made an allusion to a vacationing wife but I didn't care. I was no home-wrecker.

'This one doesn't look bad,' he said, leaning over the steering wheel of his yellow Maserati to inspect the front of the Hotel du Danube, where I would stay for a month. I often met men who owned new Maseratis when I was nineteen and twenty.

Who are you to judge a man of the world's manners? All he's doing besides spending more money than you're ever seen except in gangster movies, and rinsing your neck in wet kisses, is telling you how wonderful you are.
    'Seduce a Top Model' – French *Vogue* for men.

'What! You're applying foundation on to your naked face without first applying a protective cream?' an editor of *Glamour* magazine once said to me as if I'd just shit on the floor. Experience as teacher. I avoided it when possible. It was too difficult. Silence and observation were safer. In France it was easy. I didn't even speak the language let alone Parisian slang. I concentrated on keeping my eyes bright and wide and smiling in an embarrassed fashion – as if saying I'm such a ninny for not speaking French – but I thought what a relief! I was at my best when not moving or talking, having had hours to arrange myself at a perfect angle. As soon as you moved or talked, you had a big chance of making a mistake, which could elicit a comment. I concentrated on having static physical presence. Maybe I thought I emanated.

Paris, February 28, 1985: Today I feel strong. What makes me strong? I feel capable. Thirty-five years to feel capable, of taking care of myself and my new son. It was the new son that did it. It's not *that* difficult. You don't go on spending sprees, every successful model's bad habit, even after she's no longer successful, and you make sure he eats well and dresses warmly in the winter. My anxiety was dressing him warmly in the summer until a girlfriend told me, one eighty degree day in her sunny garden, that I was going to dehydrate, even kill my baby if I didn't take off his sweater and the blanket. And you hug him and kiss him a lot, that's easy, he's your son, a miracle, and scream at him as seldom as possible. You don't want to feel like a child abuser as well as an old model. Finding yourself a lot more tired, but basically the same nincompoop you were at nineteen, before you abdicated your beginnings of self to become a cherished image. So now I have a baby and the beginnings, it's a lot, and I feel insolently lucky to have this middle-aged chance to grow up. As if I've had my cake and will now proceed to eat it.

James's nursery school is near another of my Parisian hotels, there were four or five in all: the Nova, 82 Avenue de Clichy. It doesn't exist any more, it's been made into apartments, but the Nova café is still here. I'm in it. An ugly café, furnishings from the sixties growing older: beige, plastic-cushioned booths with missing springs and rips in the seats, still visible under thick strips of solid masking tape. Everything else is cream formica, or dark orange or dark brown. A life-size sepia photograph of a stream in a forest covers the entire back wall. A sepia-grey day in the woods, right here on the Avenue de Clichy. I'm as easily engulfed in atmospheres now as I was then. That pleases me. The dry white wrist of the *garçon* placing my café crème in front of me pleases me. His faded wine-coloured cotton jacket is strained across his skinny shoulders, and he walks like a lazy girl.

I remember the Nova Hotel better than the other hotels I stayed in during my first year in Paris because I was most alone there. I stopped seeing Pierre as I stopped seeing everyone, quickly. I spent a lot of time in my traffic-noisy room on the third floor, overlooking the Avenue de Clichy, which is planted with tall, handsome, bushy-branched trees. I remember the weather as always grey; the trees made it greyer. Even the metro, La Fourche, was depressingly ill-lit. I remember nothing bright, except the orange, phosphorescent lettering on store fronts: CLICHY 2000 – HIFI, AUDIO, WRISTWATCHES, COLOR TELEVISION GUARANTEED 5 YEARS – 275 SQUARE METERS. And in between each warehouse surface was a string of small shops with windows full of women's cheap suits and nylon underwear and beige and brown, black and blue, spools of thread and buttons. There was ASTORIA'S ENSEMBLIER for men, and the MAXI SHOP, shiny Gothic beige letters outlined in brown, a yard tall and six inches thick, detached from the store front by a rusty metal frame; for men, women, and children. And a thousand other versions of lower-middle-class ready-to-wear. Fashion-conscious as I was, I could have wept for anyone who shopped on the Avenue de Clichy. The people who lived on it all looked poverty-stricken. This was my first 'popular' area of Paris and I found it grim. I wanted to be a rich, famous model and living around here made me feel like a poor immigrant. It never occured to me that I was. But I knew I wasn't French. Neighborhood shopkeepers, when forced to deal with me buying aspirin, cigarettes, croissants, did so as if with a baseball crowd, the caricature of an entire nation. I received personal condolences for the death of John Fitzgerald Kennedy.

I arrived at Paris Planning modeling agency with a letter of recommendation from Ford's in New York and was received as if I shouldn't have bothered. After a week of appointments with the fashion magazines, fruitless except for two last-minute quarter-page reshoots for *Elle*, they stopped sending me anywhere. Now I had to remind them who I was when I called, which I'd recently stopped doing altogether. My return ticket to New York was always in my pocket and I was living off the money from the job in Spain. There was very little left. My diary entries of the time are full of fear and self-hate; I usually wrote in the afternoon after gorging on mille-feuilles and Paris-Brests and four or five croissants, facing the prospect of a lonely overweight evening.

There was another American model staying in the room next to mine, Jan from Ohio, who was responsible for my being at the Nova. I wouldn't have minded seeing more of Jan but she was always working, with the best photographers and the best magazines: Helmut Newton, Jean François Jonvelle, Harri Peccinotti; Italian *Vogue, Elle, Vingt Ans, Votre Beauté* . . . She'd rattle on in the hallway after work, a little like Jacob, assuming I knew what she was talking about, intimidatingly beautiful in full make-up, the kind of beauty men don't even dare whistle at in the street.

Sometimes we'd have breakfast together in this very café. Jan would arrive smelling of Palmolive and Patchouli and dressed to kill in an ankle-length crushed velvet A-line skirt, a peasant blouse with an adjustable drawstring décolleté, and a silk scarf as wide as her skinny arms and five times as long, wrapping her forehead, crossed in the back of her neck, twice around her throat and hanging down to her calves, bordered with tiny round mirrors like beads. I would arrive unwashed, probably in the jeans and T-shirt of the previous day. I didn't have many clothes and saved them for weekends. I was dating a count. Jan would have already been to a newsstand and read me bits from the *Herald Tribune*'s back page while we drank our café crèmes. Then I'd walk her to a taxi-stand and go back up to my room until I found a reason to leave it again. The maid wanted to change the sheets or I couldn't stand being there anymore. I'd walk around a few blocks, never venturing far from my uncomfortable haven. Visiting a museum seemed an impossible exploit. I'd buy cigarettes, shampoo, go back and take a long time washing and drying my hair. I cried a lot, which also passed the time. Crying calmed me down and made me hungry so I'd go out and buy cakes. After eating the cakes I'd feel slightly catatonic and write in my diary.

During the week I usually ate an early dinner on a stomach full of cakes, in a macrobiotic restaurant Jan had taken me to one evening. (Have I ever taken *myself* anywhere? If I had not had the great good fortune of having been taken places, sometimes I'm sure I'd still be sitting in my mother's kitchen.)

A small unmarked storefront in a tiny dead-end street. It was always full, of pale, silently chewing individuals who were either lobotomized criminals or members of a sect. But it was cheap. For seven francs you ate an overflowing plate of grains and vegetables. Jan was a great bargain hunter. Atmospheres didn't seem to bother her. (But modeling eventually did. Five years later she went into therapy with R.D. Laing.)

Once I sat directly across from a man who was drawing a fish on the paper tablecloth in time to his meal. Forty scales on his fish, forty chews in his mouth. I didn't count but I'll swear to it. Except I realized when his drawing was three-quarters finished, he'd started with the tail and worked up to the head with a stage-smart sense of suspense, that it wasn't a fish but a thick-tailed devil. The man himself had a meticulously trimmed spearhead goatee and nails filed into points. He noticed me trying to find it all very normal and shot me a sadistic smile; scared the shit out of me, which seemed to please him. From then on, I ignored him unsuccessfully and left as quickly as possible without seeming to run away. His loneliness had smelled mine and aimed for it. Like wankers on dark streets know in front of whom to open their coats.

As usual I'd been more worried about hurting his feelings than afraid he might actually be dangerous. It's one more example of how I did everything: made love to men, modeled, ate, walked, slept. To avoid disapprobation, jealousy, pain, and one step further, to receive approbation and love. Never a thought for my own desires, other than the all-engulfing need to be popular.

I was dating a count on weekends. Many young models get sucked into an aristocratic pack of playboys. They run in packs to assure themselves a live audience for their acts of bravura, drollery, and seduction. And because they can't cross the street on their own. Overbred Catholic good boys trying to be bad by fucking models.

A month previously I'd been sent to a sixty-year-old marquis by P.R., the young, up-and-coming French photographer who'd used me on the two small *Elle* jobs. Sweet P.R. laughed like a donkey and had bad posture. And was always backing me into corners and trying to kiss me, exhaling windy laughter in my ears and drooling on my neck because I wouldn't let him get to my lips. Maybe that's why he wasn't using me anymore.

Over a whiskey at the George V Hotel, I smiled and felt ill at ease – would I ever feel on top of these situations? – and listened. Marquis was imposing, tall and corpulent, a shock of white hair and an aquiline nose in a long, severe, thin-lipped face. There was still an abyss between me and them. I was still a suburban hick, even if I'd had the formative experience of a year of getting fucked in New York. No one's ever honest with you when you're young and unaccompanied in big cities. It interferes with getting into your pants. And you, the hick, waste an enormous amount of time believing the stories they tell you. And every time you change cities, the whole process starts over again, for as long as you refuse to believe that the person buying you drinks and listing a load of crap they call the career plans they have in mind for you, has anything but your best interests at heart. As long as you refuse to see the world as it is, full of con men carrying Tiffany boxes full of garbage. In any case, and in fact, fledgling models freshly arriving in cities like Paris and Milan can meet *only* degenerate older aristocrats and their rich imbecile sons, uncles, nephews, and business associates. One big happy family vying for the graces and gullibility of the latest talents from Gothenburg and Missouri. They seek us out, to the point of going to meet planes from key cities like Stockholm, scanning the passengers until they find the country bumpkin and offering to drive her into town. With a little luck it's Saturday evening. She's at his mercy until Monday morning when the banks open. He offers her a Prince cigarette once she's strapped into his Porsche, and small-talks about his Swedish brother-in-law who helps him run the family's multi-national mattress business.

Our looks flatter them. Our minds are not threatening. They discuss us while leaning on the old wood bars of their private clubs. And we, the hicks and bumpkins, imagine we are meeting one Prince Charming after another.

I understood about half of what Marquis said, which is probably about how much he wanted me to understand. Maurice's bullshit had been down to earth, a pack of lies but easy to grasp – You wanna make it? You fuck sheep – So when you ended up with a bunch of men you were grateful there were no sheep. This man's approach was elegant. He was an elegant important man. He was going to make me into the new 'Look', of an important Parisian high fashion house that even I had heard of. He would dress me in their après-ski wear and take me to Megève. I didn't know where that was and didn't ask. I assumed it had something to do with where the factories were. Did they have factories? Or all the sewing machines. He emphasized the queen he would make of me, describing her aura, her grace and crowd appeal and my obvious potential, which unnerved the hell out of me. I didn't feel up to being the new 'Look' any more than I'd felt up to being Twiggy's or Jean Shrimpton's successor. That's how they get you. You think you have to deserve the attention you don't think you really deserve.

He invited me to Brussels. I thought he must be trying me out for Megève. We stayed in a hotel palace where the personnel discreetly addressed my host by his title.

I was wearing a royal-blue A-line sleeveless dress – it was the middle of winter – in a sort of stretchy industrial fabric, with a few grease spots in the lap area I kept trying to hide with my bag. I'd changed into it hurriedly just before leaving for the airport because I thought I looked better in it than in my other A-line dress. I'm sure I looked just as suburban in both my dresses and the spots were horribly embarrassing in the company of Marquis. And it probably smelled like sweat. I didn't wash my clothes as often as I should have. I thought it was forbidden in the sink of my hotel room. I was convinced I would be reported by the maid, reprimanded by the manager, perhaps asked to leave for having dripped water on the felt rug. And placing a clean towel on the dirty floor underneath the dress seemed equally forbidden. In any case, how would I iron it? I did realize the hotel had a laundry service but it was much too expensive. One had to be rich to be clean in Paris. All the clean people I knew were. Washing my clothes in the sink was like announcing my shameful poverty. You can't afford our laundry service? You shouldn't be staying here. Me against them, I often felt like that. Me alone, David without a sling-shot (unless you count blow jobs), them as a group Goliath.

Anyway, we went up to our suite and Marquis suggested I have a bath. Then he gave me a make-up lesson, and took me shopping, anything I wanted. I chose a linen baby bonnet for a cousin back in Michigan. On to the Beaux Arts Museum, where he tried to impress on me the importance of Flemish art and especially Brueghel, and was upset with the extent of my ignorance. I told him I thought Brueghel was awful. He took me to a pub.

Drink! Eat and be merry! and the inevitable disco for the rich, old, and so well brought up they can't get down. The few who can stick out like professional performers. European upper-class lack of rhythm is downright disconcerting. It was easy to look good among them, in fact better than all of them, except for the token black whom everyone watched hated and envied. Discotheques were my favourite places back then. Musical no-man's lands, where I stopped dwelling, drank free and let loose.

I should have known Marquis was going to jump on me when we got back to the hotel, even if so far his attitude had been pedagogic and paternal. His crassness caught me off guard. But letting him, them, fill me up, had recently ceased being part of the deal. I hadn't made a decision, no one had given me advice, it just happened, you might say biologically, like serpents shedding skins, or chemically, like drinking whiskey makes you drunk. So I resisted. And Marquis insisted. It was half rape and half premature ejaculation. I knew he'd ejaculated when his pupils disappeared up under his eyeball sockets and his Bourbon nostrils squeezed shut. My lips curl remembering. Who was this little twit, right? Who doesn't know Brueghel from a bagel but nods her head to everything, drinks dinners and trips, then refuses to pay for it the only way she can. You should have been suspicious of a girl who does nothing but nods, Marquis baby. You think I should accompany you to Brussels? And aren't we soon going to visit the factories in Megève? Who am I to contradict the suggestions of an experienced man? Wasn't this only a thin slice of the moon you mentioned? But who did I think I was? Had I expected separate rooms? Imagining I could come along for the ride without getting penetrated because a nobleman is noble. I didn't think, certainly not about the new 'Look' I'd never be, while he pinned me down and panted in my face. We had both miscalculated my survival instincts, which had nothing to do with a modeling career but with my new low tolerance to disgust. Who was this old fogey anyway, making an abstraction of my humanity to get his rocks off? Someone important? So is my ass baby, you've just convinced me, and you look better in your expensive suits. Jesus! I've known enough self-absorbed ejaculating cocks to ruin the sex life of an insensitive girl. Some part of me used to be insensitive to smell, taste, and touch, so I'd watch their pleasure which looked like pain, like a porno film on top of me. It was a real education in mind over matter but if fucking's not a sin then it shouldn't be a penance. I can no longer offer my body like a sinner offers prayers.

The next morning I felt guilty and he played, replayed, father. He sent me back to Paris after arranging a modest room for me in the five-star hotel of a friend of his. If I needed anything I could ask for the director. Or another friend of his, a white Russian and permanent resident of the hotel. It sounded like a set-up. As I hadn't done it with Marquis, was he going to do me this big favour and in the meantime have me so closely watched I couldn't do it with anyone else? But because of my guilt I obeyed him. Marquis stayed on in Brussels.

The permanent resident invited me to lunch long before I needed anything. He took me to the Bar des Theatres, one of the all-time favourite bistros of the 'tout-Paris', with two titled landowners and a sexy Swedish blonde. One of the landowners, shy, short Count Jérôme, a young divorcé, asked me to dinner that evening and took me home with him. Marquis's friend and watchdog was obviously informed of the late-morning hour at which I'd returned. He paid me a visit in my small plush room to gently scold me and accuse me of acting like a man. So it was a set-up. I didn't know how to explain that I wasn't acting like anything, I was reacting to and uncomfortable in my new sophisticated surroundings and the blue-blood macho standards which governed them, where even more than in the streets I didn't know my ass from a crack, and no one was around to teach me because the rules were secrets among men. Didn't I realize (it was impossible I didn't appreciate) my great good fortune, coming under the protective wing of an important rich nobleman, suburban bimbo that I was? No, I didn't realize I was being kept. I was paying fifteen francs a night for my room. It never occured to me that in a five-star hotel that was a token to protect my pride.

When I was a twelve-year-old hypocrite, sinning nightly in my bed while attending St Norbert's school for good Catholic children, I acquired the nasty habit of passing 'dirty' notes in class. Bad-breathed Mr Brightness, my lay teacher, dutifully intercepted one of my salty missives and kept me after school, sat next to me in a student's desk like mine, and leaned in close. Did I know what 'bastard' and 'son of a bitch' meant? I didn't, I simply appreciated their effect. He leaned in closer. I leaned away and kept breathing out violently. Being alone with my teacher in the unnaturally silent school and his unnatural proximity, the amplified noise his saliva made in his mouth when his dry lips parted, the sandpaper sound of his chin stubble inside his papery palm, the clicking of his blinking eyelids, the foulness of his breath, convinced me forever that the words I'd used were very disgusting, as disgusting as Mr Brightness's breath, and I never forgot it.

Mr Brightness waited a long time for my answers, while I listened to his noise and tried to think of something not 'dirty' to say. He was breathing too hard to risk provoking. He didn't think it proper to correct what I finally said.

Marquis's friend was staring at me like a loving bird of prey, perhaps waiting for my confession, yes, I fuck everything I see. (Whatever else one did back then one always fucked. It was the age of fucking one and all, and if you didn't participate in the orgy, born of birth control and beatniks, hippies and feminists, if you weren't an all seasons, all times of the day and anything goes nymphomaniac, something was wrong with you.) I didn't move and I didn't say anything, convinced that whatever came out of my bad girl's mouth would be stupid or used against me. I changed hotels the next day, after meeting Jan from Ohio at my agency which was also hers.

'Give me a little hope, rat-face.' David Bailey must have said it at least once, if not a thousand, five hundred times, to every model he's ever worked with. Must be ten thousand of us. I like to think he knows how hard it is in the beginning of any shy girl's successful career, to be up to the beauty we've been turned into for the day. That that was his perverse way of commiserating. He always said it while arranging, scratching – whatever men do with their balls. Then again, he may have a hard time living up to his own image at times, which has more to do with reality than make-up, shadow and light – London East-End street-smart and well known wit, wicked as the glint in his eye that undresses you while he gently cuts you to pieces, laughing, making you laugh. It's the least you can do, be an appreciative audience, even if the target of his jokes is yourself. Who can be funny all day in a void? There must be days he doesn't feel like trying, but maybe, like a model thinks she always has to be pretty, he thinks he always has to be funny. People certainly expect it of him. Maybe he really needs the hope he continually asks for.

'Give me a little hope, rat-face . . .' by being as beautiful as you know how, I think you're beautiful or you wouldn't be here, he'd say that, and I'll make you more beautiful than you thought you could be. Think about fucking, rat-face. He never said that, to me anyway, but it was as if he had. Or did I only imagine it? *Oh* did I imagine it. Wanting to fuck makes modelling very easy. The 'fuck-me' expression is the most sought after one. No, wanting to fuck makes modeling very interesting. Fake-wanting-to-fuck makes it easy. I'd known how to fake fuck from the word go; it came naturally; I was fabulously successful at it. Fake-wanting-to-fuck-for-pictures took me a while to learn. I had a naive idea in the beginning that you had to feel the sentiment that went with the expression on one's face. Sexual expressions have always been the most difficult ones for me, especially when working with someone I fancy. So David Bailey wasn't the easiest person for me to work with, but definitely one of the most interesting. He is one of the shameless, nostalgic, die-laughing sweetnesses I remember when I remember (rarely) what it was like being successful. I wrote letters to him in my diary: 'Dear D.B.,' which boyfriend at the time found and read over the phone to his best friend. 'Dear D.B.,' became the standing joke until I changed boyfriends, which I did more often than I changed photographers.

If my snoopy boyfriend's pride had been hurt, he didn't let on. When living with models doesn't work out, men can hide behind a mocking of models as contemporary icons not to be taken seriously. They can 'every man Jack' us and forget us. It was as if I'd written letters to Cary Grant or Elvis Presley; same adolescent mentality. Except I worked with my teen idol, and getting his autograph wasn't an impossible dream.

There were fleeting intimate friendships with other girls. Getting to know each other like detailed maps, participating in each other's dressing-room transformations, street anonymous to Diva. It took hours. We re-made the world and decided each other's futures. What became the intolerable déjà-vu of those conversations was often the best part of the first five years. Which is about how long a model's career lasts. It's rare to have modeled for as long as I have, maybe a hundred girls, no more than two hundred, have modeled for more than ten years and for twenty, maybe only ten. God bless our stolen souls.

David Bailey and a handful of other giants (Guy Bourdin, Gian Paolo Barbieri, François Lamy) were our incestuous and make-believe papas, uncles, brothers, beaux, pick a straw, rat-face darlin', g'on . . . we'd continue our beautiful people day over dinner, then go and close the discotheques, sleep little, and start again early in the morning if we'd stopped at all, if we hadn't spent all night changing rooms, emptying each other's mini-bars and making love not war. The circles under our eyes were proof of our *vécu*, made us even more attractive. Our hangovers honed our wit.

What was truly marvelous became terrible as I became aware of how little I was in control of what was happening. The satisfaction of reaching a goal you've set for yourself doesn't work in the case of modeling; it's too manipulative. The art directors, photographers, make-up and hair people, the magazine editors, have reached a goal, packaging a marketable product, you and everything smudged on and hanging off you, and you've let them. The successful model's satisfactions, other than her bank account, have not much to do with a job well done, rarely get beyond infantile wish fulfilment: you're so cute, you're so funny, you turn me on, me too, you look great in that shiny pink lipstick, I'm hungry, I'm thirsty (we're immediately fed and given alcohol), what are you doing tonight, let's go boogie! Or let's go shopping! . . . I'd danced and posed and laughed and drunk myself into a clay-muddy ditch because that was the most exciting way to do it, like a jet set society member, I'll bet we have more fun, and that's the *only* way to do it, if you care about a job well done.

I don't look my age. Which is great. But the girls got younger and I started doing every job like it was the last. And what am I still doing here? But it's stupid to refuse all this money, haven't got enough to stop making it, go to school for four years . . . I observe as if from an impassable distance a process which began approximately fifteen years ago, with refusing four out of five jobs a day, and 'ended' with making courtesy calls to clients and not paying my rent. It never really ends, there's always the occasional free job for a friend, I just did a job for a cigarette ad, made twelve thousands francs in two hours. It's the first job I've had in six months.

No one ever officially retires you and hands you a gold watch for services rendered, what service do we render except to our narcissistic selves? WE'RE VERY GENEROUS WITH OUR MONEY. I once asked my agent for a gold watch when he asked me if I ever planned on stopping. Is he trying to tell me something? Why don't agents ever have the balls to come out and say it. It's curtains on your career in chic, S. They know better than to hope we'll figure it out by ourselves, and even if we do, that we're capable of walking out on what was our life and our entire self-image until then, to start a new life with the no plans we've made and the no money we've put aside. There's no retirement fund. So what are your projects, S.?

There's a large Samsonite suitcase full of yellowing magazine pages and jokes and 'beauty' gone, sour indigestion and a series of broken hearts which convince me I'm incapable of a stable private life.

So why the hell did I want it so bad? I don't know, for all the wrong reasons when they seemed like, maybe even were, the right ones. I not only didn't mind being manipulated, it suited me, I called it being taken care of. The no money now was lots of money before. The photogenic beauty I turned against even before people stopped asking for it was the incomparable satisfying discovery of that beauty: A DREAM COME TRUE . . . what young girl is indifferent to the proof of what she hardly dare suspect and desperately, yes desperately, hoped for, but on one knew or gave a shit – she was no longer the lonesome ugly duckling but the mythical swan, gliding across glossy pages and *Vogue* covers for all the world to see, admit, admire, *suck in their breath*! On my back and around my neck and tear-dropping off my lobes, the most expensive clothes and jewelry *in the world*, made up and coiffed by the best hairdressers and make-up artists *in the world* . . . photographed by the best fashion photographers *in the world* . . . BECAUSE I AM ONE OF THE MOST BEAUTIFUL GIRLS IN THE WORLD! even if I have to drink four glasses of whatever there is in the studio to feel up to the task. *It was worth drinking for*. That's the crux of it. The narcissistic cooing over ourselves that people think makes up 90 percent of model's modeling, why people hate us and are jealous of us and they're right, it's positively orgasmic. Except it happens at the very beginning and is shortlived.

You get over the shock of being thought beautiful and it gets easier and harder before it gets only hard. Easier to talk to people because your new 'beauty' has made you less shy and wary of the importance of beauty, even of its reality – how beautiful are you without the products on and the lights shining? Your revenge against the Cherry Hill Homecoming Queen doesn't feel as good as it should. And more and more difficult to model because, manipulation aside, picture perfect beauty is a monumentally boring thing to be and re-be every day.

Ask ten models what they do for a living and watch five out of ten hesitate before telling the truth or lying. A girlfriend of mine once introduced herself as Dr Audrey Matson at a wedding reception on Long Island:

'*Susan*! all the men wanted to introduce me to their mothers! It was wonderful! I got more respect in an afternoon than out of ten years of modeling!'

Belgium, October 7, 1985: Here I sit in my cosy hotel room in Knokke-Le-Zoute, next to the casino where the show will be held this evening, erasing my heels and elbows with Dr Scholl's dead skin cream, making myself perfect, more and more perfect, so perfect my heels and elbows will bleed – yes! waiting for a fatal phone call. Do they want me? Am I good enough to wear Armani? Or are they afraid I'll show up with flabby forearms and a wrinkled neck. I saw them over a week ago and you never know at my age, the signs set in fast.

I'd just spoken to Italy from the phone downstairs:

'Can I call Milan?' I'd asked the teenager behind the desk.

'Can't you call from the casino?' He looked threatened.

'I don't know, I haven't tried.'

'Milan, that's in Italy?'

'Yes!'

October 8, Sunday morning on the train: Knokke-Le-Zoute – Brussels, from where I will fly to Milan. Fitting today at noon.

The show last night was an ornate, kitsch experience: a big stage and two small stages on either side, one of which I occupied, brushing my hair and daydreaming in my boudoir decor, overflowing, the boudoir and my person, with chiffon, lace, silk, powder puffs, and various other Dior products, and framed by a gold-painted pseudo-Chinese screen behind which I disappeared to change awkwardly, twelve times. The other small stage was occupied by musing Magritte (René), alias Dominique the mime and my male counterpart, symbolizing the lover and artist. I don't think I symbolized anything but Dior, oh yes, and the muse. The middle was reserved for ten girls who tangoed, waltzed, sleep-walked, modern danced, jazz danced, and shimmied, in nightgowns, body stockings, silk stockings, bras and panties and garter belts and merry widows – while Jane Birkin whined and whispered: Les Dessous Chics – the elegance of that which is underneath.

In between each choreographed number, Magritte and I would do our thing. I'd powder my nose or read a blue letter, he'd mix a colour on his palette or clean his brushes, he'd *write* a blue letter, in fact I read it afterwards (he'd made a long list of obscene words), I'd glance at him and blush – while a cassette played, of me speaking my own sentences about men (I hated the sound of my own voice but one always does and I couldn't wince in front of the audience, nor laugh at the long list of obscene words), and French actor Philippe Leotard, with his cigarettes-and-tequila-for-breakfast voice, read Magritte's thoughts on women and art.

It was pretty damn sophisticated for an underwear show. In fact it may end up being the most sophisticated underwear show of all time and it was no doubt sadly misunderstood, wasted, on the Knokke-Le-Zoute crowd. The original owner of the casino was a good friend of the real Magritte; the casino's dining room walls are covered in famous frescoes; the show's theme wasn't difficult to come up with.

Showing my no tits, flat ass, and bunioned feet to an attentive crowd wasn't easy in the beginning, I never do underwear, no one asks me, but around mid-show I started relaxing, almost enjoying being almost naked on a stage. I mean it's all up front and see-through, you may as well exhibit what you can't hide.

Slept three hours last night. I close my eyes and immediately start dreaming. My ankle, cramped, moves itself out to stretch, and encounters an obstacle which moves forward. I jerk awake and my ankle jerks back, defeated. I 'hear' the obstacle looking at who is probably its mother, the latter sitting next to me, and open my eyes to find mother and daughter staring at me like a strange animal. The mother titters, for no reason I can think of unless I have shit on my face. Christ I hate provincial mentalities.

Getting off with my over-prepared suitcase, two days or two weeks, I take the same houseful, they watch me having a hard time, the train compartment is full of paralyzed men; smiling, know-it-all.

'Have a nice day!' I say with emphatic good humour. They return my salutation with small twin whines. I can't help myself. I add, just loud enough for the occupants of the nearest seats to hear: 'You have,' I point, 'shit around your mouth,' and turn away as their hands fly up.

Milan, noon: From the back seat of my stopped taxi, I watch a tall thin Italian in a small crowd of people watching a race. A blonde on a bicycle rides past and he follows her course, momentarily forgetting the race. While you watch that blonde's receding behind, an available woman is watching you from behind your back. I swear I wish I had the courage to just go up and introduce myself.

Corso Armani: Mustard-brown and rust-orange walls, armadillo roofs, Mediterranean sky . . . out of the center, Milan is a deserted postcard. The vision of this quiet street fills me with quick sharp happiness. I want to sit on a bench and cry maybe. Fill myself up with it. There's no bench so I stand and breathe deeply, thinking, I'm often defeated simply because there's no bench, when in fact, these are some of the moments I remember most vividly, years and years later, gazing too quickly at scenes I don't generally see.

Armani has his own theatre in the round, horseshoe rather, with comfortably cushioned and cushion-backed seats. Padded muffled walls, and probably bomb-proof sheets of steel beneath the padded muffling. It's all underground, air-conditioned, nicotine-filtered. To get to the elevator which takes you there, you pass through an enormous courtyard parking lot laid with strange but pleasant rubber flooring, perhaps recommended for the maintenance of Rolls Royce and Daimler tires. And a bullet-proof glassed-in reception booth enclosing a stoop-shouldered male concierge, and a snot-ass peroxide receptionist who asked me what I wanted as if she were the secret mistress of the proprietor (who owns majority holdings in several mega companies as well as this, his Milanese pied-à-terre), and I was a tresspassing tramp. You feel like you are about to enter the elegant hide-out and central computer control of James Bond bad guys. My instinct is to karate shave Miss Snot-ass, her mud-thick foundation, but I control myself.

Didn't talk during my fitting, my smiling clothes-tree best. We rehearse tonight at six-thirty.

Three o'clock, the 'Fiera': A gigantic carton-walled space without air, where most of the shows will be held because most designers aren't rich enough to possess private bomb shelters.

Looking around or making the effort, I feel too self-conscious to notice much. Even though I have pinned on my chest the same official-looking badge as everyone else in here. I keep waiting to be asked to leave: NO SMOKING SPITTING RUNNING URINATING BARE FEET DOGS OLD MODELS.

Young dynamic model booker David suggests I:

'... hang out in the Patisseria, heavily made up.' That one of my grandmother peer group was landing two or three shows a day that way. Call girl to street walker, right Dave? I feel undignified being here at all.

Hotel Fiera: Why did they put me in such an expensive place? Because you can't afford not to be in with the 'in' crowd, S., don't complain. My roommate George (a girl) from New York, born while I was graduating from high school, paid three hundred thousand lire, three hundred dollars, to work out for a week at a local health club. Defined musculature and wide shoulders, like the thin boy stylists who dress us, are more important these days than being pretty. Yes, I promise I won't smoke in the room.

Five o'clock tea and beer, Hotel Fiera bar: Lisa Rutledge, Tracy Lee, Rita, 'les girls', drinking on marshmallow leather couches around a low table. In model generations I'm two up on them, feel like I've been sitting in this lobby all my life.

Overly-thin Rita says she's been:

'. . . vaccinated for life,' as far as agents go, having recently left a long time lover-agent. She's nineteen, started a while ago, at thirteen, fourteen maybe. Is lover-agent the one who got you hooked, beauty?

'See you around,' she says languidly, a bit later, as I wait for a taxi and she goes up to her room. An ugly woman next to me follows Rita's progress into the elevator, turns to the ugly woman next to her and says:

'Didn't she work for you?'

'Yes,' says the second ugly woman.

'You can't say she's beautiful,' continues the first, 'you really can't say she's beautiful.' Bitterly, in French. It's not that it never crossed her mind that perhaps I understood. As another model, I guess I still look like one with my make-up on, I am taken less notice of than the waiter who'll toss her dandelion stems this evening. Jealous bitch. She'd love to be languid and get away with it. Rita is one of the most beautiful girls in a beautiful girl business.

'It's not feminine, it's really not feminine,' the first ugly woman concludes, content, staring at the closed elevator doors as if she wished Rita could hear her.

'I'd rather you didn't speak of my friend in front of me,' I announce, in French.

'Excuse me?' the first ugly woman looks up at me, frightened.

'Frustrated bitch!' I walk away, trembling a little.

'Hi! I'm Bill Ford. I've seen you around somewhere.' Looking like he'd just taken a shower in the fraternity house, a young man addresses me in the bar where I'm still waiting in the taxi line. I introduce myself and we shake hands solidly:

'Your mother Eileen picked me up at a bus-stop in New York fifteen years ago.' He looks aghast.

Armani rehearsal: many models and most of them new, except me and a few other diehards.

Looking themselves over after seeing each other in magazines, checking out each other's bodies. All 'stars', who never work together because stars work alone, except during the major shows. New York stars, Parisian stars, everyone flies to Milan, then Paris, then New York, to be seen in good company and get richer. Twenty shows, an average of five hundred dollars a show, in one week, in each city. Sixty times five hundred equals thirty thousand dollars in three weeks, minus expenses, many of which are taken care of, and agent's percentages. Stars pay less because they work more, 5 percent instead of the beginner's 20 . . . it's worth the short-lived exhaustion. And a few of them get a *lot* more, like ten or twenty times more, than five hundred dollars a show.

Armani Fashion Lab: Everyone's been alloted mandatory white technician's coats. We're about to test beauty products on a public who've tried everything.

No urinating unless accompanied, no smoking, (this afternoon it was fiction and paranoia, tonight it's for real) no personal jewelry, that includes wedding rings and Rolex watches and ankle bracelets, no personal belongings of any kind, of course that includes bags dear, anywhere near you.

They clutter the collection. A room has been allocated for our possessions, which which will then be locked until the rehearsal is over. May no one need a tampax for the next four hours. What? A pillbox? You have a *heart* condition! *Madonna*, did your agency know this when they let us book you?. *Liebchen, Divinity*, I'm so sorry for you, we cannot afford, I'm sure you understand . . . sick specimen . . . give me your coat dear, the white coat, that's right dear . . .

Pep talk by Armani before going on:

'If you think this is a rehearsal, you're *wrong*.' It was marked 'rehearsal' on all the official fashion week calendars of events.

'There are four hundred of my best clients out there. It is *very* important.' He pauses for effect, then throws us a joke.

'Do it like a Valentino evening dress,' and beams expectantly. An assistant standing a little behind and two heads lower down – Armani is a short man standing on a tall box – bursts out laughing. A few models take the hint and titter.

'Excuse me if I am nervous,' he continues. Humble no less. He doesn't look nervous to me, he looks like Joan of Arc before battle. And a little like a Pekinese dog. Facing him on the level, or is it because he's always got his chin in the air, lets you see everything in his nose's furry interior.

'Go out there and *smile*, with your *teeth*. But *tough*.' Now we're getting to the nitty-gritty. Smiling *teeth* as opposed to eyes and/or mouth. Carnivorous. Got'cha Babe. You're a marketing genius. A girl next to me remarks, impressed:

'Can you imagine the power this guy has, putting up "no smoking" signs and people *obey*.'

The four hundred important clients must have been pep-talked too. They systematically applaud everything. You can barely hear the Muzak.

Walked to La Rigalo for dinner with Peggy P., 'face of '84', Venezia, an Italian-American brunette and a South African girl whose name I can't remember. I love the precise English of South Africans.

It was full of playboys, ones I recognize, ten years later, with younger girls. Tan old men with faces furrowed from sun, drugs, drink, and bad sex. One of them met my eyes and looked distressed, sat down at his table with his back to me. He couldn't place me but I reminded him of when he could still come.

The face of '84, a picky eater, working in her image from the inside out:

'May I have a receptacle to pour out the excess oil?' Never finishes her plate, a personal asceticism.

'I can't sleep on a full stomach.' She goes on and on about how a tasty healthy meal makes her as happy and satisfied as anything she can think of. Like fucking? Maybe she's never heard of it. Can you sleep with a dick in you? Or does that too give you that full feeling and prevent you from sleeping?

'But is it possible to calculate the magnesium content? To know how much you need? Isn't there a risk of taking too much?' At the end of her meal, I can see her filling in to the straight lines of her chair, a faultless rectangle, happy as a new dress.

Back at the hotel, agents prowling the lobby bar. A Swiss agent, blonde, plump, tipsy, is complaining about the arrogant French who refuse to send their best girls to Lausanne. Keeps interrupting her rambling tirade to address the back of her hand – crack! – to each person on her blacklist. Seven times in ten minutes counts Jean Louis, my French agent. Jean Louis loves his girls. His eyes moisten when he describes his favourite passages in shows.

'And to you too!' she concludes, addressing Jean Louis as if to say don't think you're not as bad as the rest of them. Her fist just nicks his chin, precise drunken timing. She's getting dangerous, dwelling on the beauties whose percentages escape her. Jean Louis listens patiently, amused, knowing if he doesn't contradict her she'll go to bed soon.

Short square Enrico, in charge of the shows at my Italian agency, ambles over, addresses me as a comrade:

'What you care about money? We are rich interior. Other people, they have nothing inside, they need rich exterior.' Then he scolds me:

'I told you. Eight years ago. Look at Pat Cleveland. She has a hundred thousand stashed, even more.'

'I'm not Pat Cleveland, Enrico. Eight years ago I thought I was over the hill. I already thought no one would book me. I was afraid to come. I had to wait until it was *really* too late, so if I worked it would be a miracle, and if I didn't, it was normal, I could feel detached. So I'm detached, so detached I feel stupid for being here.' Enrico looks at me and shakes his head sadly.

Smoke a cigarette in the toilet and fall asleep next to my healthy roommate.

October 9: Wake up thinking, this is all very interesting but it isn't. I'm too old to be here, I'm as old as the playboys. I want to know women my own age. I love the young girls, they're lovely, funny, not always naive, a lot of them already don't respect their job any more than I do; but they keep making me forget I'm ten, fifteen years older than they are because in my head I suppose I'm not. Something's wrong with me. I miss my son. I want to go home. I want to get out of this expensive hotel where I'm doing shit-all anyway, inspecting the stucco architecture. I trust morning feelings.

Nine-thirty, in front of the Fair Hall: *Women's Wear Daily*, the high-priest fashion critics, arriving in cemetery-black stretched limos, to watch the shows of the designers they are here to kill and bury and rarely, to praise.

Think of all the thousands of jobs you have absolutely no memory of. Think of all the people you see who say hello and you can't remember who they are and how you met them.

> It's backstage in the wings at the Thierry Mugler show that I meet Susan Moncur, top model, long silhouette, smooth skin, star of St Laurent, Cacherel, and many more – drowning her fear in overflowing champagne flutes:
> 'I always drink before the show. It's easier that way. Because the people are animals, animals in a zoo, each more horrible than the next. I hate them with all my heart. It would be better to slaughter them all, and if I didn't drink I'd slit their throats instead of model.'
>
> Patrick Amory, *L'Evenèment de jeudi*,
> article on the ready-to-wear shows.

Standing on tiptoe next to Jean Louis, watching the Versace show, watching the beautiful animals as I'm usually watched. Surrounded and being made deaf by photographers' motor drives, jungle rain, and disco sex tunes booming out of building-size speakers loud enough to hurt; my shoulders, my lungs, are being beat on. But it's getting to me. I feel like dancing. We're gorgeous. We walk gracefully. We look down at the public condescendingly. We have great asses, great tits, great legs, and we have rhythm. Eat your hearts out, slob voyeurs.

Across the aisle, a century-old man is leaning forward on his cane, gripping its ivory and gold knob with both hands, wishing it were his dick, bug-eyed, tense.

Vanilla caresses her breasts when she stops to pose but never stops moving. Another girl scrapes a flat hand across her sex before it lands on her hip, to slow blues. I've done similar things with the help of champagne. (How many shows have I done without? Two? Three?) It's the extension of what is demanded of us. Contained lust. We're more exciting than strippers, who undress themselves. We are dressed and undressed by other hands, passively acquiescing, making whatever they want to do to us easy for them.

Alison, a wild mane of red hair and painfully white skin, always walks angrily, like she was on her way out. I keep waiting for her to jump off the end of the podium, rip off the clothes and dump them on the nearest magazine editor's head, shouting obscenities, and run naked and free into the streets and back to Miami where she hides out between seasons. She gave a farewell-to-the-business party two years ago but keeps coming back. She was sunburned and fatter the first time she returned and worked less than usual. Designers don't appreciate mental and physical health, the antithesis of the long suffering anorexic lust they're used to and thrive on. Who was she to decide she was fed up with them before they decided to throw her to the dogs?

Rita is really too thin but so gorgeous, and she moves well. I didn't ask her about the drugs, I don't know her well enough, but maybe she needs someone to ask her if she really feels like dying at twenty-one? Does she think she won't move well without them? Then again who am I to moralize, who can't step on to a podium without my half bottle fix, without making sure I'll float right through it.

Watching Vanilla closely, she's truly amazing. She gets into it, becomes it, uses breaks in the music to improvise beautifully. She has a terrible, tragi-comic reputation, shows up regularly for shows she's not booked for and refuses to leave until someone gives her a dress. And it works. Designers are flattered or get embarrassed and end up giving her one to avoid a scene. Then she asks for another and another, or takes the ones she wants off other girls' clothes racks. And once out on the podium, she won't get off, spends three times longer up there than any other girl. She's either a megalomaniac nut case or smarter than all of us. I 'interviewed' her once on an airplane; she described herself as Yves St Laurent's wife. I decided she was a nut case and threw out the notes for humanitarian reasons. But I'm not so sure. In any case, she's a damn good show model.

Monique is too shy. I identify with shy girls and feel like shaking them. Shyness looks terrible up there.

Kirat is also too shy, but that comes from thinking herself too old, which is a shame because she's better than a lot of them and the look in her eye kills it. Does she see all the shows she's ever done passing in front of her eyes and freak?

Red, so haughty and contemptuous offstage, looks tremendous up there looking haughty and contemptuous.

The finale works well although I'm not sure I get the point. Red comes out in a pastel Sunday suit and a spotlight, walks petulantly to the highest of three platforms, spotlighted all the way, opens a small crocodile handbag and gropes for a smaller pink-and-white nosegay, snaps the bag shut, and more and more petulantly, walks back and straight through a line of waiting, suited men. The bride? Must have been because Gianni Versace appears, bowing, saluting, half-rock star, half-archbishop, and walks triumphantly down to the end of the podium with Red on his arm, to thunderous applause. The other girls, Vanilla first, run out and freak-squeal behind the happy couple as is the custom, applauding with their arms in the air, elbowing each other to get at Gianni's cheeks, painting them fuchsia with photogenic kisses.

> Gaby, freckle-faced Irish New Yorker, grateful member of AA, cried all day yesterday: 'I did fittings, it's so degrading. I'm going to cancel Claude Montana. He makes me nuts. His make-up hurts me. I don't need this shit . . . anyway, today I'm making an abstraction of all that . . .' She speaks warmly, an arm tight around my waist, which for the second time that morning brings tears to my eyes. 'I'm not bitter!' I wail, 'I've simply been doing this damn job for too long.'
> 'Show Notes' – article in fashion exhibition catalog, Georges Pompidou Museum.

Girls arriving in the agency afterwards, one by one. My roommate George:

'I always get so depressed after the show, it's so nerve-wracking. How did I look? He really likes me. He gave me four changes. *All* those *important people* you see out there *staring* at you . . .' looking frightened, wanting to be reassured. I empathize but it hits me from another angle for once, having just watched and being full of our 'power', the pure power of the powerless.

Gaby arrives next, complaining about the agency never calling her anymore in the morning to ask if she'd slept well. I inform them, with much enthusiasm, of their 'power', and they look at me with big eyes, wanting to believe, but they don't trust the judgement of one of their own. And what was an old hag like me even doing here in the first place, spying on them from the audience? You get some weird people hanging around you when you're a model, sidling up, trying to touch you, get your telephone number, become your instant best friend, pretending to be new designers, new photographers, agents, movie producers, aristocrats. Or not even pretending to be anything, hangers-on, depressed, jealous, unfunny 'fans', who announce their problems and ask for advice, then hold it against you because you're pretty and they're ugly. They call themselves hopeless and they are because they can't get beyond nature's injustice. What can you say in the end? Life's tough. Had I gone weird? After having been a model, had I become a model groupie who couldn't live without the hot rush of fashion six months before it hits the streets? What was the alternative? Hiding out in a squat, balancing back and forth on a chair that doesn't rock, eating compulsively, not even despairing, just nuts? Puzzle of a Downfallen Child number ten thousand and five. Or spending all my time in Swiss spas paid for by an older fogey than myself, getting tummy tucked, tits lifted, goat-embryo injections, DNA capsules, and whatever other fountain of youth treatments the rich, paranoid, unhappy, and aging, spend their money on? (*Which* older fogey? Marquises and Maseratis don't like you any more, S.) I've always wanted to be a social worker. You have *not*.

And whichever one of those things my younger sisters were thinking, what difference did it make? It would never happen to them. I never thought it would happen to me. My presence slightly embarrassed them. Why hang around a show hall when you're not doing any shows? I'm doing Armani. Oh. I slightly embarrassed myself. I'm writing a book. Oh yes. Everyone knew. I talked about it compulsively for a few years before I finally, compulsively, started taking notes. Everyone sees me doing it. A few people even think I'll finish it, wish me luck. Gaby is writing a book too. So are many other models, thinking they'll keep the 'power' and the 'glory' as well as getting the immense satisfaction of telling it like it is because so many people tell it like it isn't.

Non-smoker George says, still deep in the throes of her latest appearance in front of fashion's power structure:

'But when I saw that girl on video, I was thinking, God, I wish I had the guts to do that.' A voluptuous model had done a little improvised shimmy number on the high platform which had been greatly appreciated backstage. Because not only the audience, but all the other girls and the designer and his multitudinous assistants, make-up people and hairdressers, watch you fuck up or 'get down' on a video screen behind the curtain.

'I thought she looked ridiculous,' I said. 'In fact, no one in the audience applauded. Even from way back where I was, the natural movement of the hips and shoulders is already so much, all you need is the look in the eye.'

'Yes,' counters George, 'but she did it for the video and on video it worked. It's the video that counts, the people have gone home now.'

'Oh, of course, I forgot . . .' whole new world, the people don't count, the video counts. Christ I feel old all of a sudden.

Gaby said she'd been interviewed by ABC afterwards.

'What kind of questions?' I ask.

'If you were speaking to someone you'd never met over the phone, how would you describe yourself?'

'That's a terrible question. What did you say?'

'I was still undressing, I was practically naked, they were filming me, without permission of course, right? So I stood up, bare tits, it was a woman asking the questions . . . "I don't know, what would you suggest?" '

'Serves her right. What else?' I want to know everything, all the details, theirs and mine, theirs to prove mine.

'They asked: "What's the nicest thing about the shows?" And I said: "The fellowship between the girls." ' I went up to Gaby and hugged her. Two years ago she hugged me, I can't remember why. I think we were both crying. Everyone cries during the shows.

Talk with a professional show photographer during lunch. I throw the power of the models on the podium at him and he looks sceptical, a short, young, fat man from New York:

'I look at it like space to fill. I'm being paid thousands of dollars to be here. I wait for the girl, I wait to have the dress well-framed, I look for eye-contact, you only have a split second . . . I don't care about the rest. I'm not attracted to the girls sexually. I don't find them sexy. But visually, it's interesting.'

Why do men feel obliged to defend themselves against our deaf-mute beauty if they're convinced we're a sexless mirage?

Hanging around the hallways: Editors are wearing Azzedine. Models are wearing Azzedine. Everyone in the business wears Azzedine, self-consciously, like mis-cast Carmens.

Spying on Mila Schon: A terrible show. The lights are murder on the girls' faces, and it's not just because some of them are too old to be up there. I'd be up there if someone'd asked me. We would all be gorgeous in seaside restaurants with older men, which is where I wish we all were.

Everyone's trying too hard and looks unsure of themselves. Gaby is smiling like someone whose top row of false teeth have just come loose and if she unclenches her jaw they'll fall out on to the podium in front of two thousand people.

When you don't push to get up front, like my bitchy dancer friend up there, when you're not placed in an important position by the designer, you drown. I'm watching people drowning. Anne Marie, my bird-faced friend from New York, is breezing through, wind in her skirts. Looks great. This is the only show she's doing, the only chance she has to prove herself for next season. And maybe she's like me. I'm often good in terrible shows. When I'm not intimidated by the superstar structure of a Versace, a Lagerfeld, a Gaultier, where I feel my every step, wobbly turn, expression, to be a test of whether or not I'm good enough, I feel responsible. Like someone needs me to be good. It becomes a singular endeavor, being good when everyone else is bad. Even Red's not trying. She looks insecure. Didn't know she could.

Traffic jam at the end of the podium. Bump cars. Watching this terrible show, I see, feel, taste, the harm, for the ten millionth time. Some of them will think it was their fault. Nothing's ever our fault. Only Vanilla's always good.

I see the same 'keep you pride' tic I've noticed in myself, in Beverly Johnson, waiting in a group to walk down – the slight lifting of the chin, and again. Will soon be over, dear.

Another girl is scratching her ass while waiting in a crowd of ten wearing the same style dress in different colors. Thinks no one can see her because she's not spotlighted. Liebchen, in a show like this, you're the most interesting thing to watch.

Bitchy dancer just shot the audience a shoulder up Betty Boop from the back. Yuk! There are not only men out here, honey.

Beverly Johnson had a passage to herself and looked stunning, even with an Ali Baba gold lamé turban on her head, which on any of the other twenty girls in this show would have looked like part of a grade school play costume. Vanilla is posing after her own passage, having a hard time leaving as usual, watching Beverly's progress, looking sick.

Gaby is the bride. It's always nice to to be the bride, even in terrible shows. Everyone applauds you because you signify the end.

Mila herself appears, a battle-worn parade horse, as the audience gets up to leave. They must applaud now that she's here so she gets a standing ovation. Gaby kisses her twice; nice.

Another girl sticks her face out to give Mila a smooch on her return from the end of the podium, but Mila doesn't see her coming, walks into her and gets punched in the jaw by the girl's cheekbone. Poor Mila reels.

Wounded, I am wounded by all this.

In the Fiera toilets: Sticker in front of me where I sit – JUMBOROLLE – carta igienica, toilet paper, papier hygiénique – and a drawing of an elephant's ass from the back.

October 10, 4:45 p.m., Milano Centrale: Oh, I couldn't have spent two more nights in that hotel anyway, with a roommate who doesn't smoke.

I missed the damn train. I haven't missed a train or a plane in years. My upper lip is twitching. My jaw feels like it's about to lock. I keep stretching my mouth open (gasping for air) to make sure it still opens. Lack of what vitamin? Shit, I could have asked Peggy but now I won't be seeing her.

Armani cancelled me, voilà, I've said it, I've been avoiding writing it down.

Ricardo (my Italian agency's proprietor) broke the news, an arm around my shoulders:

'And I have some bad news for you.'

'Armani cancelled me.'

'Yes.'

'Oh.'

'He cancelled fourteen girls. We had a meeting.'

'When did you find out?'

'This morning.'

'Why didn't you tell me this morning?' He shrugged, bending his head to one side and making small circles in the air with a hand, fingertips touching, arm bent at a forty-five degree angle.

'We had a meeting.' He repeated. What could he say? I wasn't going to ask him why. For once I didn't feel like turning the knife in the wound. He wouldn't have told me anyway, if some designer's assistant had seen a grey hair glistening under the lights, or one of my crooked teeth smiling unesthetically, on video, or because someone had said I walked hunched over and it's only attractive on Terry Toy (who walks hunched over to keep his long blonde hair covering his five o'clock shadow); or I'd done it like a Valentino evening dress and he was only kidding . . .

'But I'll give you everything he gives me, five thousand francs for the rehearsal . . .'

'You mean the audition.'

'. . . and he will pay for your ticket and your hotel.' Yeah, fashion popes can afford to buy you and then pay you to leave. A quick heavy sigh escaped me and I realized I was about to cry. Tears welled up. But I thought I was so detached! Unemotional tears welled up.

'It's normal, it's O.K., it's normal,' I kept repeating, half to myself.

Anne Marie lent me her ray-bans, for which I was grateful. The lighting in the Fiera is awful, not only on show podiums. I wasn't about to walk down those hallways, even once, with my old, blotchy, cancelled face, foundation and powder striped in tear rivulets, uncovered, for all the world to see. Or would I have enjoyed it? No. And it's not the whole world, S.

I told Ricardo I would leave Milan the next day, walked back to the hotel incognito and drank two beers at the pope's expense, then returned to the Fiera to watch that terrible show with perfect lucidity. I could have left immediately but I guess I came here for this to happen. I wanted to savour it, not miss a minute, even prolong, my own defeat. I wanted it to sink in. I've been waiting so long. The pope made it possible and he will kindly pay for my last night. He won't even notice. I'm a rhinestone sparkle in his bucket of rubies.

Maybe I'm simply afraid of being forgotten. Of course I am. Of being unloved. But none of those people ever loved you, dummy. Yes they did. In their own way. They told me often enough. But it wasn't me, it was themselves.

Crossing the busy main thoroughfare between the show hall

and the hotel yesterday, I caught myself walking slowly and watching the cars coming at me fast, thinking at the same time, I know you're naturally dramatic but this is nuts. It was like a compulsion, like I couldn't help myself, the cars were coming at me and something was sucking me toward the cars. I'm nervous, have been called hysterical, anxiety-ridden, approaching terminal exhaustion and afraid of my own shadow, but I've never once thought of myself as suicidal. Life *is* full of surprises.

Maybe there's nothing waiting for me the day there are no more jobs at all. I wouldn't wear your bride's dress if you begged me. I don't want to face 'The Abyss'. But I do! You *are*, S. Good old Ricardo felt so sorry for me. That didn't help. I've forced him to be the bringer of bad news, to shove me in. But it's right it was him. He'd been designated sixteen years ago – the day he invited me for a drink at his hotel in Paris. When I walked in he was standing like a magician waiting for applause next to the bar, which he'd draped in posters of my first *Vogue* cover.

December 12, 1985: Brady's café, killing time. Isn't that a funny way of saying it? 'Killing' time until dancing class.

Three-quarters finished (three-quarters killed) with *October Ferry to Gabriola* by Malcolm Lowry. His theme of dispossession – isn't that what I'm talking about in all my notebooks, on every page, without ever having realized? I'm trying to dispossess the model (who's already been dispossessed by one after the other of her clients, there's very little room left to breathe), meanwhile having forgotten, perhaps I never realized that either, that the model dispossessed the woman long ago in order to exist as successfully as she did. And if I 'kill' her, what other proof of existence do I possess? Was there ever a woman? I was a model child and a model adolescent. I followed rules, not always unhappily. Then I was lost for a short time, yes, the beginning of a woman, then I was offered the moon. I became, gratefully, an irreproachable lunar image.

A model mannequin. Now I'm lost again. Floundering. No moon, no rules.

But isn't that wonderful? Christ, all I need is a job. For the rest it's wonderful, even if there's a little more pain coming... I'm getting fed up with my pain. Make my own moon and rules. One day at a time.

> 'Brown hair, clear eyes, Susan is American. Thirty-six years old, five foot nine. According to present criteria, she is too old and too short.'
>
> Interview by Fabian Gastellier, *L'Unité*.

Founded in 1986, Serpent's Tail publishes the innovative and the challenging.

If you would like to receive a catalogue of our current publications please write to:

FREEPOST
Serpent's Tail
4 Blackstock Mews
LONDON N4 2BR

(No stamp necessary if your letter is posted in the United Kingdom.)

Also published by Serpent's Tail

The Seven Deadly Sins
Alison Fell (ed.)

'Seven fine writers, seven vices probed to the quick. Splendid.' ANGELA CARTER

'These seven writers represent... a newer and more knowing feminist strategy . . . Mischievous and exhilarating.' LORNA SAGE, *The Observer*

'Rich in experiment and imagination, a sign of just how far contemporary women's writing might go.' HELEN BIRCH, *City Limits*

'All of these stories cut deeply and with a sharp edge into the main business of life — death, God and the devil.' RICHARD NORTH, *New Musical Express*

'A rich but random survey of recent women's writing.' JONATHAN COE, *The Guardian*

'An exciting, imaginative mix of stories.' ELIZABETH BURNS, *The List*

'Witty, modern, female.' KATHLEEN JAMIE, *Scotland on Sunday*

'Extremely entertaining.'
EMMA DALLY, *Cosmopolitan*

Also published by Serpent's Tail

Sex and the City
Marsha Rowe (ed.)

'Unerringly entertaining and thought provoking.'
JOANNA BRISCOE, *Girl About Town*

'The whole book opens into the category of good dirty fun, and is not the worse for that.'
ROBERT NYE, *The Guardian*

'A mixture of 1980s eroticism, sexual humiliation and an underlying wistful longing for the milk of human kindness, seemingly destroyed by urban living. Compulsive stuff.' *The List*

'Strangely intriguing.' *Glasgow Herald*

'There is no other collection quite like *Sex and the City*.' *TES*

Also published by Serpent's Tail

From Sleep Unbound
Andrée Chedid

'Andrée Chedid tells this story as though she were a jeweller assembling a bomb; her precision and grace (and those of her translator) are remorseless.'
HARRIETT GILBERT

'*From Sleep Unbound* captures not one woman's world, but that of *all* women, whether ... cloistered and closeted in a society bound by retrograde customs or in a modern metropolis, liberated for all intents and purposes, but imprisoned within their own psychological cells.' BETTINA KNAPP

'A brilliant, touching book.'
VICTORIA BRITTAIN, *The Guardian*

'A passionate study of life imprisonment.'
JENNY DISKI, *New Statesman*

'Chedid's spare but beautiful prose makes of this uneventful life a moving parable of oppression and the human spirit's capacity to fight it.' *7 Days*

'A deep, poetic meticulous exploration of the mind and history of ... a woman who liberates herself by killing the husband who has tyrannized her.' *TLS*

'Chedid's beautiful tale is a timely reminder that the freedoms Western women take for granted concern them alone.' *City Limits*

160 pages £4.95 (paper)